SAMPSON TECHNICAL COLLEGE

NORTH CAROLINA
STATE BOARD OF EDUCATION
DEPT. OF COMMUNITY COLLEGES
LIBRARIES

P9-BTX-949

QUALITY OF LIFE IN OLDER PERSONS

HQ
1061
G38

QUALITY OF LIFE IN OLDER PERSONS
Meaning and Measurement

Linda K. George
Lucille B. Bearon

Both at
Duke University Medical Center
Durham, North Carolina

 **HUMAN SCIENCES PRESS**
72 Fifth Avenue   3 Henrietta Street
NEW YORK, NY 10011 ● LONDON, WC2E 8LU

Copyright © 1980 by Human Sciences Press, Inc.
72 Fifth Avenue, New York, New York 10011

All rights reserved. No part of this work may be reproduced or utilized in any form
or by any means, electronic or mechanical, including photocopying, microfilm and
recording, or by any information storage and retrieval system without permission in
writing from the publisher.

Printed in the United States of America
0123456789 987654321

Library of Congress Cataloging in Publication Data

George, Linda K
   Quality of life in older persons.

   Bibliography: p.
   Includes index.
   1. Old age. 2. Social indicators.
3. Psychometrics. 4. Gerontology—Research.
I. Bearon, Lucille B., joint author. II. Title.
HQ1061.G38   305.2'6   LC 80-13645
ISBN 0-87705-488-6

This book is dedicated, with affection and respect,
to our parents.

CONTENTS

PREFACE

Age in a virtuous person, of either sex, carries in it an authority
which makes it preferable to all the pleasure of youth.

> —Sir Richard Steele
> *The Spectator,* No. 153,
> August 25, 1711

Cato requested old men not to add the disgrace of wickedness
to old age, which was accompanied by many other evils.

> —Plutarch
> *Cato the Elder*

Old age: blessing or curse? This question seems to be one of the
mysteries of the human condition. For centuries, renowned
thinkers have debated the relative advantages and disadvantages of late life. Today, social scientists, policy planners, and
service providers add new perspectives to the controversy as
they strive to understand and improve the quality of life of older
people.

In this book, we—as social scientists—have addressed the issue of how to conceptualize and measure the quality of life of older people. We have designed a concise reference work which documents the "state of the art" of measuring life quality in terms useful for gerontological research, planning, and practice. More specifically, the book (1) presents a conceptual context for the assessment of quality of life, (2) introduces a set of criteria to use in selecting a measuring instrument, and (3) describes and evaluates in detail twenty-two measuring instruments in terms of psychometric properties and conceptual and methodological issues.

This book is intended for researchers, people involved in designing, implementing, and evaluating programs for older people, and others interested in improving their understanding of social science research in the field of aging. In order to be useful to a broad audience of researchers and practitioners, we have strived for a rigorous, but non-technical style of presentation.

The decision to write this book was based on our conviction that adequate measurement is a critical phase of the research process in that the quality of the research findings is contingent upon the quality of the measuring instruments. The book thus has developed from our commitments to improve the quality of aging research, to promote the translation of research findings in terms useful for planning and practice, and, ultimately, to the development of rational and knowledge-based programs capable of improving the life quality of our older citizens.

ORGANIZATION OF THE BOOK

Chapter 1 addresses conceptual and definitional issues relevant to the study of quality of life in older people. It includes our definition of quality of life, the specific dimensions we have

included in our instrument reviews, and is critical to an understanding of the categories of measuring instruments subsequently reviewed.

Chapter 2 presents a brief and non-technical discussion of
issues important in assessing the adequacy of measuring instruments. This material will be more important to those persons
new to the research process, but also develops the standards
used in subsequent chapters to evaluate available measuring
instruments.

Chapters 3 through 6 review the classes of measuring instruments suggested as dimensions of life quality for older people. Chapter 3 addresses measures of life satisfaction and
related concepts, Chapter 4 examines indicators of self-esteem
and related concepts, Chapter 5 reviews measures of general
health and functional status, and Chapter 6 examines indicators
of socioeconomic status. Each of these chapters includes an
essay which describes relevant conceptual and measurement
issues. The specific measuring instruments reviewed are selective, chosen to represent the best available, the most frequently
administered, or the historically most important measures. No
claim is made for an exhaustive presentation. Instead we have
attempted to describe and evaluate the most relevant instruments currently available.

The final chapter briefly summarizes the major themes of
the volume, presenting conclusions about measuring life quality
and suggesting fruitful areas for further instrument development and refinement.

We have tried to assemble this volume so that the chapters
and the reviews of instruments may stand independently and
maintain their meeting. We remind the reader that the first
chapter, however, is essential to an understanding of the classes
of instruments subsequently reviewed. We encourage the reader
to selectively sample the materials or to review the volume as
a whole, whichever is most appropriate to his or her background and interest.

Acknowledgments

The quality of this book has been greatly enhanced by the contributions of several colleagues. The chapter on self-esteem certainly reflects the insights and assistance of Linda Breytspraak. Gerda Fillenbaum provided valuable insights to our discussion of health and functional status. Richard T. Campbell, Angela O'Rand, and Leonard Gionet provided essential assistance to our consideration of socioeconomic status. Additionally, the book as a whole has benefited from the comments and suggestions of George L. Maddox, M. Powell Lawton, and Robin Karasik.

Deborah Coley, Pam Hass, Karen Young, Cecilia Teasley, and Rosiland E. Thomas typed this manuscript and deserve special thanks for their patience, good humor, and skill. Norma Fox, Editor of Human Sciences Press, provided helpful editorial and production assistance.

We are especially grateful to the Andrus Foundation of the National Retired Teachers Association and the American Association of Retired Persons, who provided financial support for the preparation of this volume. We have benefited not only from their financial support, but also from their commitment to the translation of research findings into terms useful for older citizens.

Chapter 1

QUALITY OF LIFE: CONCEPTUAL ISSUES

   Throughout history, people have written about
"the good life." While the details of their
descriptions of the good life may have differed,
probably all would have agreed that man strives
for material and spiritual well-being. In many
ways, "quality of life" is a modern counterpart
to the notion of the good life. Like the good
life, quality of life is an attractive and appealing subject, bringing to mind personal im-
ages of pleasure and contentment as well as
riches.

   On the whole, social scientists have failed
to provide consistent and concise definitions
of quality of life. The task is indeed problematic, for definitions of life quality are
largely a matter of personal or group preference; different people value different things.
To illustrate, consider Tibor Scitovsky's
unique and picturesque notion of the items
which are important in assessing quality of

life across cultures, as depicted in Table 1.1.
Scitovsky rather humorously concludes that Americans' quality of life is somewhat lower than
that of western Europeans. But the comparisons
in fact may be highlighting differences in cultural values rather than differences in perceived
quality of life.

Social scientists are interested in patterns
rather than idiosyncracies and have used two
primary categories of variables to define quality
of life. Some authors have defined quality of
life in an objective, status-oriented manner,
examining personal characteristics such as assets,
health status, and financial security (cf. Gastil,
1970; Morgan and Smith, 1969). Other authors
have defined quality of life in terms of the subjective evaluations that individuals formulate
about their own life experiences (cf. Campbell,
Converse, and Rodgers, 1976; Andrews and Withey,
1976). In this volume, we view both objective
measures of resources and status and subjective
evaluations of personal life experience as important dimensions of life quality. Certainly,
the quality of one's life appears to encompass
more than adequate material well-being. It also
includes perceptions of well-being, a basic
level of satisfaction or contentment, and a
general sense of self-worth. Thus, we suggest,
both objective conditions and subjective evaluations are important considerations in the assessment of quality of life. Using a distinction
made by Campbell, Converse, and Rodgers (1976),
life quality includes both the conditions of
life and the experience of life.

TABLE 1.1

Indicators of Quality of Life:
United States versus Western Europe

	United States	Western Europe
Fresh fruit as a percent of all fruit consumed	62%	87.2%
Fresh, frozen, or smoked meats as a percent of all meat consumed	66%	90.5%
Average minutes per day devoted to walking, hiking, playing outdoors, and engaging in active sports	7.9 min.	28.5 min.
Percentages of adult population taking annual vacations of six or more days	27.7%	44%
Average time spent alone while awake per day	6.6 hrs.	4.1 hrs.
Average minutes per day devoted to gardening and pets	3.3 min.	16.8 min.
Expenditures on flowers as a percent of national income	0.20%	0.39%

DATA FROM: Tibor Scitovsky, The Joyless Economy.
    New York: Oxford University Press, 1976.

WHY MEASURE QUALITY OF LIFE?

Quality of life is an organizing concept of potential importance to all who work toward improving the conditions of life--basic scientists, applied researchers and service practitioners. In addition, the broad appeal of this concept should help to facilitate communication between knowledge-oriented and action-oriented professionals. Let's examine specific ways that quality of life has been or can be used as a meaningful construct in research and service delivery involving older people.

Basic Research

Social gerontologists have conducted considerable research geared toward answering the question, "What is successful or optimal aging?" (cf. Cumming and Henry, 1961; Havighurst, 1963). Historically, investigators focused their efforts on describing social patterns of aging. More recently, they have begun to delineate the conditions under which aging is satisfying or debilitating and to identify the resources and coping skills which influence the aging process (George and Maddox, 1977; Lowenthal, et al., 1975). In a sense, these investigators have used measures of quality of life to depict successful aging and the conditions associated with particular patterns of aging. Using quality of life as an organizing concept, basic researchers can continue to make positive social contributions by developing knowledge about late life in terms meaningful for the action-oriented professional.

Applied Research

Gerontologists involved in applied research have directed most of their attention to assessing the status and needs of the elderly and evaluating the impact of particular service programs or policies on older individuals. Much of this research implicitly aims to improve the life quality of older people (or at least certain needy target groups of the elderly), and some research explicitly proposes to do so (Hausmann, Feldman, Hundert and Davis, 1974; U.S. DHEW, 1972).

Planners and administrators often set modest goals for their ameliorative programs and expect improvement in only certain domains of their clients' lives. Nonetheless, these focused programs ultimately should contribute to overall improvement in quality of life. Therefore, quality of life is a central concern of evaluation researchers who typically examine the broader, and perhaps latent, impacts of social programs.

Service Delivery

Practitioners are directly involved in the planning, implementing, and delivery of service programs for older clients, and are committed to the most effective methods of providing these services. Understandably, then, practitioners frequently express their goals in terms of improving general life quality or the quality of conditions in a specific life domain. Further, it is the practitioner who often has most direct access to reports of the rich and complex life experiences reported by older people. Thus, the

concept quality of life can provide the practitioner with a rubric for interpreting the reports
of clients they serve and provide a link between
their activities and those of the basic or
applied researcher.

Quality of life is thus a concept which serves
the interests of the basic scientist, the applied
research investigator, and the service practitioner. It has relevance to both soical science
theory and social policy. We are now prepared
to move beyond the issue of why to measure
quality of life to a consideration of how to
define it in terms of measurable domains.

DEFINING QUALITY OF LIFE:
FOUR SELECTED DIMENSIONS

For the purposes of this volume, we define
quality of life in terms of four underlying
dimensions, two of which are objective and two
of which reflect the personal judgment of
the individual. Table 1.2 presents a list of
these dimensions.

TABLE 1.2

Dimensions of Quality of Life

Subjective Evaluations

    Life Satisfaction and Related Measures
    Self-Esteem and Related Measures

Objective Conditions

    General Health and Functional Status
    Socioeconomic Status

Our restriction to these dimensions is admittedly
selective, but we believe that these dimensions
are especially central in assessment of the quality of life of older people.   In fact, we see
them as crucial components of life quality in
this society in general.   We do not claim, however, that when these four dimensions have been
measured, the investigator has fully assessed
quality of life.   Instead, we view these as four
dimensions out of a potentially infinite number
of aspects of quality of life.   We do view them
as sufficiently important in the scheme of American values to be considered virtually universal
components of life quality in this society.
Some conceptual issues regarding these selected
dimensions will be briefly discussed in this
chapter; more detailed conceptual issues as well
as measurement issues will be addressed in subsequent chapters.

The Dimension of Life Satisfaction

Perhaps the most crucial subjective assessment
of life quality that indivduals can report is
their relative satisfaction with life in general.
For example, in a large national survey, when
asked specifically about the quality of their
lives, individuals tended to respond in terms
of their degree of satisfaction with life in
general (Campbell, Converse, and Rodgers, 1976).
Both researchers and practitioners may wish to
know whether older people are satisfied with
the ways their lives have progressed, the situations they find themselves in now, their future
prospects, and whether they are generally happy
and have a sense of well-being.   These kinds of
information help to capture the richness and
variety of life experience.

Indeed, social gerontologists have accorded much attention to issues of life satisfaction as a dimension of life quality. The major theories of successful aging have been formulated with life satisfaction designated as the outcome of interest. Both activity theory (Lemon, Bengtson, and Peterson, 1972) and continuity theory (Maddox, 1968) discuss aging outcomes specifically in terms of "life satisfaction." Likewise, disengagement theory (Cumming and Henry, 1961) identifies outcomes in terms of "morale," one of a number of closely related concepts which will be discussed in Chapter 3. In gerontological research, hundreds of studies have addressed the issue of the relationship between aging and life satisfaction, making it "perhaps the oldest, most persistently investigated issue in the social scientific study of aging" (Maddox and Wiley, 1976, p. 15).

The Dimension of Self-Esteem

A second subjective dimension of quality of life is self-esteem. Self-esteem is typically defined as a general sense of self-worth—a belief that one is basically a person of value, acknowledging personal strengths and accepting personal weaknesses (Wells and Marwell, 1976; Rosenberg, 1965; Coopersmith, 1967). Self-esteem is thus a self-evaluation and cannot be ascertained by an observer. Related concepts include self-regard, self-acceptance, self-concept, and self-image. All of these concepts share an emphasis upon the individual's assessment and evaluation of himself or herself as an object (Crandall, 1973; Wells and Marwell, 1976).

Available evidence suggests that positive
self-esteem is an important component of general
assessment of life (Andrews and Withey, 1976).
Self-esteem may become increasingly salient with
the transition from middle to old age (Schwartz,
1975). Most self-esteem theorists, (e.g., Wells
and Marwell, 1976; Rosenberg, 1965) suggest, with
supporting evidence, that self-esteem is developed and maintained through a successful process
of personal interaction and negotiation with the
environment. To the degree that environmental
changes accompany the process of aging, self-
esteem must be renegotiated. Further, to the
degree that successful negotiations with the
environment are less likely in late life, the
self-esteem is less likely to be positive. This
suggests that age-related events and stresses in
late life may alter the older individual's self-
esteem. This perspective, as well as the importance of a sense of positive self-regard, has
led Schwartz (1975) to describe "self-esteem
as the linchpin of quality of life for the aged."
Thus self-esteem appears to be a useful indicator
of subjective quality of life.

A more careful examination of this concept in
relation to service programs might be enlighten-
ing. Practitioners and applied researchers
might note the importance of assessing a person's
self-esteem during and after assistance. Bloom
(1975) suggests that social service programs,
while performing the intended function of providing assistance, may have unintended detrimen-
tal effects on the client's sense of self-esteem.
That is, in the process of receiving services
earmarked for a clientele that is in some sense
regarded as "needy" or "helpless," certain individuals may report increasingly negative

self-evaluations. Thus, receipt of services may
not be accompanied by a corresponding increase
in the subjective perception of life quality.

General Health and Functional Status

General health and functional status are, by
and large, objective conditions which are important components of quality of life. Although
physical well-being is undoubtedly an important
life condition for all members of society, health
and disability appear to be particularly salient
to the older population, as evidenced in (a) the
significantly higher incidence rates of chronic
diseases among the elderly, (U.S. Public Health
Service, 1972), (b) the increased length of time
most older individuals require in order to re-
cuperate from acute illnesses (National Center
for Health Statistics, 1971), and (c) the impressive degree to which health is mentioned by
older survey respondents as a major life concern
(Louis Harris and Associates, 1975). The most
frequently reported dread of older persons is
that health problems or disability will interfere
with their capacity for independent living
(Hoffman, 1970; Louis Harris and Associates,
1975). Indeed, fear of illness-related dependency surpasses fear of death among older individuals (Jeffers and Verwoerdt, 1969; Riley and
Foner, 1968). Thus health is an important dimension of life quality and is a cherished resource
for the majority of adults.

Health, in spite of the fact that everyone
probably has a common sense notion of its meaning,
is often defined in broad, ambiguous terms unsuitable for systematic research purposes (De
Geyndt, 1970). Following the initial lead of

the World Health Organization (1946), most recent definitions of health include the element of positive well-being as well as the absence of disease, discomfort, and disabilty. For the purposes of reflecting quality of life for older people, functional status is perhaps the most important aspect of physical well-being and includes such factors as mobility, ability to perform self-maintenance and preferred activities, and general energy level. Functional status is both an indicator of life quality for older adults and a resource which conditions the subjective experience of life.

Objective data concerning functional status and general health can be collected using one of two major methods. The first method is to have qualified health professionals (i.e., physicians) assess and evaluate the physical well-being of the individual. The second method is to have individuals report their illnesses, activity limitations, and other specific health events.

As previously stated, general health and functional status are considered largely objective phenomena. However, it is possible to use a slightly different approach and to ask subjects to rate their own health (i.e., as good, fair, or poor), instead of asking them to report specific health events. This approach taps the subjective dimension of health, and such ratings are conventionally referred to as ratings of self-perceived health.

Both objective and subjective measures of health and functional status will be included in the review of instruments. We view health and functional status as largely objective components

of life quality, but wish to include subjective
perceptions of health since there is evidence
that the latter influence behavior and attitudes
(Tissue, 1972; Maddox and Douglass, 1973).

Socioeconomic Status

Adequate income, material well-being, financial security . . . these phrases may be the
first that come to mind when one considers the
term, "quality of life." Certainly we agree
that the material conditions of life are important components of life experience. It is less
clear, however, precisely how economic conditions
contribute to life experience. For example, do
financial assets operate such that the more one
has, the better one's life experience? Or, instead, does a threshold exist, such that the
individual whose assets fall below the threshold
is virtually sure to suffer, while those persons
whose financial resources exceed the critical
value may or may not experience a general sense
of well-being? Thus, while we are confident
that material adequacy is a component of quality
of life, we are unsure of its relative magnitude
of importance and of the process by which it
operates to condition life experience.

Reports of amount of income, occupation, kinds
of assets, educational attainments, and patterns
of income sources are used as primary measures
of socioeconomic conditions. This supports our
view that socioeconomic status is generally
treated as an objective phenomenon. However,
like health, material well-being can also be
assessed subjectively in terms of perceived
adequacy of income, satisfaction with financial
resources, and so forth. In that there are no

standardized measures of subjective socioeconomic
status, we have restricted our review to objective
measures of socioeconomic status.

Many existing programs provide either direct
financial aid to needy older persons or services
which offset financial costs in the consumer
marketplace (e.g., health or nutrition services
provided on an ability-to-pay basis). When
evaluating or planning income-related service
programs, it is important to consider the total
configuration of financial resources including
both the source and amount. For example, recent
Social Security increases, while intended as a
benefit to older recipients and largely operating
as such, also had the unintended consequence of
raising the income levels of a significant minority of older persons to the level where some persons became ineligible for Aid for the Aged or
other services they had previously received on
the basis of their "low income" status. Thus,
some individuals received an increase in Social
Security payments, but received no net financial
gain since they simultaneously become ineligible
for other financial services. In these cases,
the sources of income changed while their overall
financial resources did not.

There is surely little doubt that financial
conditions are one core component of quality of
life, and they will be included in the review of
measuring instruments.

SUMMARY

In this chapter a conceptual scheme of the
components of quality of life has been presented.
Quality of life is depicted as both an objective

and a subjective phenomenon, including both the
conditions and the experience of life. The suggested components of quality of life are: life
satisfaction, self-esteem, general health and
functional status, and socioeconomic conditions.
These components are viewed as important to
basic research, applied or evaluative research,
and to service delivery. A particular component
may be more appropriate to some research questions
than to others.

Each component was briefly highlighted in terms
of definition, significance, and relevant conceptual issues. In subsequent chapters each component will again be examined in terms of measurement
techniques and conceptual issues which influence
the choice of an optimal measuring instrument.

Chapter 2

CRITERIA FOR EVALUATING THE ADEQUACY OF
MEASURING INSTRUMENTS

Any type of research--from the experimental
tasks of laboratory scientists to the qualitative
evaluations of clinicians--is inherently at the
mercy of the quality of the measuring instruments
used in the research process. Phrased bluntly,
the data, and hence research results, are only as
good as the instruments used to gather the data.
Unless investigators can have confidence in the
instruments used, they cannot have confidence in
the results generated by their research projects.
If inappropriate or poor quality instruments are
used, researchers cannot determine whether negative results (or a lack of significant results)
are due to inadequate theory and hypotheses or to
the inadequacy of the instruments.

In basic research, the need for adequate measuring instruments is clear and well-documented
(Selltiz, Wrightsman, and Cook, 1976). Adequate
measuring instruments are also crucial in the
design, implementation, delivery, and assessment
of service programs. This position has been

15

persuasively stated by Gordon and Morse (1975):

> All too often evaluation studies con-
> tain no suggestion of the quality of
> measures being used to assess a program's
> impact. . . The lack of sensitive,
> validated, and reliable measurement
> instruments limits current attempts
> at evaluation. This lack will be par-
> ticularly costly if, as appears likely,
> many programs encounter ceiling effects
> with regard to how much change can be
> induced with a given level or resource.
> With limited resources, the impact of
> a program may be rather small; though,
> on a large scale, its impact on behavior
> and life styles would be meaningful.
> Without measuring instruments capable
> of making fine distinctions, it is
> likely the potential impact of such
> programs will not be correctly assessed.
> (p. 343)

A diligent researcher can typically find a
measure of any particular social-psychological
or attitudinal variable she might wish to tap,
given time and energy to search available literature. The demonstrated quality of these instruments, however, is likely to vary widely.

A number of criteria against which to evaluate
the adequacy of any instrument will be discussed
in the following pages. But, in this volume,
with its emphasis on research with older adults,
one criterion deserves special attention: adequacy of the instrument for use with older samples. It is important to realize that an instrument which has been demonstrated applicable to

specific age groups or to the adult population in general may not be equally appropriate to older people. Two relevant factors which distinguish older from younger people are chronological age and cohort membership.

Chronological age can be an important factor in the measurement process because a given instrument or measurement approach may not be equally appropriate to all age groups. For example, considerable evidence indicates that reaction time (i.e., length of time between presentation of a stimulus and response to the stimulus) increases with age (cf., Botwinick, 1967). Thus, an instrument with a time limit might not be an "age-fair" test. That is, across different age groups, scores on such a measure include differences in reaction time as well as differences in the phenomenon of interest.

Cohort membership, usually determined by date of birth, refers to the relatively unique historical and compositional features of a particular group. Those persons who are currently old have had different historical experiences than younger persons (i.e., the experience of the "Great Depression"). This class of experiences, known as cohort effects, may affect responses to measuring instruments, making particular instruments unequally suitable to persons of different cohorts (Riley, 1973; Schaie, 1965; Mason, Mason, Winsborough, and Poole, 1973). Education is one example of a cohort effect known to bring about patterns of differences between older and younger subjects. Younger cohorts have substantially higher average levels of education than older cohorts for a number of reasons, including changed social expectations about desirable levels of

education and changes in the amount of formal
education typically required in the job market.
This has at least two implications for research
investigators. First, the researcher should note
that differences between older and younger subjects on some measures (e.g., vocabulary test
scores) may reflect differences in educational
attainments (a cohort phenomenon), rather than
differences due to the aging process. Secondly,
the researcher should be careful to phrase measuring instruments (e.g., questionnaire items and
their instructions) in terms easily understood by
persons with little formal education so that the
measures are applicable to all members of the
sample.

The investigator need not eliminate instruments
untested on older subjects. Rather, the investigator should use such instruments carefully, acknowledging their limitations, and indeed should
shoulder the responsibility of demonstrating that
the measures are also adequate for use on older
subjects.

TYPES OF INSTRUMENTS

Most of the instruments reviewed in this
volume represent one measurement approach--they
rely on the self-reports of subjects in an interview situation or in response to a self-adminis-
tered questionnaire. Other measurement approaches
include the use of archival records (e.g., medical
charts, school records) and the observation of
behavior in laboratory or natural settings. Each
approach has its limitations and strengths (for
a review of these issues, see Selltiz, Wrightsman,
and Cook, 1976), and there is some evidence that

the optimal measurement strategy is to measure the same phenomenon using several different approaches (Campbell and Fiske, 1959).

Self-report measures are essential for investigators of quality of life because of the need to obtain subjective assessments about the experience of life as well as objective information about life conditions. Self-report measures have been successfully used in both basic and applied research. One reason they have a broad appeal is because they are quick to administer and require relatively little interpretation by the investigator. In addition, they are relatively "portable," permitting administration in a number of settings (although there is evidence that situational factors or characteristics of the setting may influence some self-reports).

Self-report measures may take a variety of forms. For the purposes of this volume, measures will be described using the same system of definitions presented in Table 2.1. These definitions represent conventional classifications of measuring instruments (cf., Selltiz, Wrightsman, and Cook, 1976).

Scales are generally preferred because they contain a larger number of items and are suitable for mathematical calculations using summed and weighted scores. The adequacy of scales also can be more easily assessed. Single item measures are least preferable because it is doubtful that one question can effectively tap a given phenomenon and because it is difficult to assess the adequacy of a single item instrument.

TABLE 2.1

Definitions Used to Classify
Measuring Instruments

Label	Characteristics
Single-Item Measure	A self-report instrument which uses a single question, rating, or item to measure the concept of interest.
Battery	A series of self-report questions, ratings, or items used to measure a concept. The responses are not summed or weighted. A battery is like a series of single-item measures, all tapping the same concept.
Scale	A series of self-report questions, ratings, or items used to measure a concept. The response categories of the items are all in the same format, are summed, and may be weighted.

CRITERIA USED TO EVALUATE MEASURING INSTRUMENTS

In this section, seven criteria used to evaluate the adequacy of measuring instruments will be briefly described.

1. Adequacy of Samples. Both the size and the composition of the samples that have been

used in the application of a particular measure need to be examined. If an instrument has been administered to a large number of subjects who possess heterogeneous social qualities, the instrument is expected to be more applicable than if only a small number of subjects or a homogeneous sample has been used.

In terms of age, optimal instruments are those that have been demonstrated to be applicable to all adults. Such instruments may be used for several purposes: to examine differences within an age group, differences between age groups, and longitudinally to examine age changes. Some research questions preclude the development of instruments applicable to the general adult population. Questions about retirement, for example, are likely to be age specific in application. In most cases, however, a concept is theoretically meaningful across the range of adult ages, but application to date has been limited to particular age groups. In these cases, efforts are needed to expand the demonstrated applicability of the instrument.

When possible, investigators should choose instruments that have been administered to broad, representative segments of the population.

2. Normative Data. Normative data provide a description of how scores on a particular measure are distributed in a population or subpopulation and often include other descriptive information (e.g., mean values, amount of variation). The generalizability of the normative values depends upon the breadth and representativeness of the samples on which the normative data are based.

Normative data are extremely useful to research investigators in evaluating the adequacy of their samples. Researchers can compare their results to established norms and determine the degree of comparability between their sample and the broader population. In most cases, the investigator wants a representative sample in order to generalize from a relatively small sample to the larger population. If the sample does not compare roughly to the normative data, the researcher has two choices. Additional subjects may be selected to yield a representative sample. Or, subjects' responses may be weighted in order to generate a distribution more similar to the normative one. The recent Harris Survey of the Myth and Reality of Aging, for example, used a weighting procedure to generate an age, race, and sex distribution similar to that of the general United States population (Louis Harris and Associates, 1975). For a thorough review of sampling theory and application, see Kish (1965).

In other cases, investigators may use discrepancies between their samples and normative data to pursue specialized research or service delivery questions. It is possible to identify important subgroups of the population by the significant differences between sample scores and those of the broader population. Using this method, policy developers often pinpoint "target groups" in need of specific services. It is usually substantially more economical to identify and serve the specific subgroups than the whole population, a large proportion of which is not in need of services (Sze and Hopps, 1974; Hyman, Wright, and Hopkins, 1962).

Thus an investment in the development of normative data is worthwhile. Normative data are useful for assessing the representativeness of a sample and identifying particular subgroups of the larger population.

3.   <u>Quantification</u> and <u>Discriminability</u>. The best measuring instruments are those that yield quantitative values and which make fine distinctions among subjects (Nunnally, 1967).

Quantification is the degree to which response categories can be accurately and meaningfully numbered. Table 2 describes the four types of data which can be coded using numbers. Nominal data are not quantitative at all; if numbers are used, they only serve as labels. No mathematical computations can be performed on nominal data.

Ordinal data are rank ordered data. No assumptions can be made about the distance between numbers. Consider the runners of a foot race, for example. If we know the order in which the runners cross the finish line, the runners have been ranked in terms of speed. We cannot infer, however, that the person who came in first was twice as fast as the person who placed second. Only limited mathematical operations can be performed upon ordinal data.

Both interval and ratio data are quantitative and have equal intervals between numbers. For interval data, however, zero is arbitrary, while in ratio data the zero is absolute. In interval data, the distance between five and six is the same as the distance between one and two. It cannot be assumed, however, that two is twice as much as one because the zero point is arbitrary.

TABLE 2.2

Four Types of Data Which Vary in
Degree of Quantification

Type of Data	Characteristics	Examples
Nominal	Numbers are merely classification labels; have no quantitative meaning. No underlying numerical order or meaning. May not be used arithmetically.	Numbers on football jerseys, religions, geographical regions.
Ordinal	Numbers are used to rank order responses along a continuum. Neither an absolute zero nor equal distance between numbers may be assumed.	Winners of a race, Moh's scale for mineral hardness
Interval	Numbers indicate relative quantity, equal intervals between numbers. Absolute zero cannot be determined.	Fahrenheit temperature
Ratio	Numbers indicate absolute quantity, equal intervals between numbers, zero is absolute.	Kelvin temperature, height, weight, cardinal numbers.

To use a familiar example, twenty degrees Fahren-
heit is not twice as hot as ten degrees Fahren-
heit. Ratio data have an absolute zero and are
most flexible since any mathematical operation
may be applied appropriately.

The most rigorous methods of data analysis
require quantitative data. When possible, measures which yield interval or ratio data should
be used. However, relatively recent methods of
data transformation permit even nominal data to
be made quantitative for purposes of analysis,
without loss of the measure's original meaning.
(For a review of "dummy variable" coding, which
transforms nominal data to a form appropriate
for quantitative analysis, see Kerlinger and
Pedhazur, 1973.) Nonetheless, meaures which
yield ratio or interval data are most convenient.

The ability to discern fine differences among
respondents is also an important characteristic
of the instrument. In general, the finer the
distinctions that can be made across subjects,
the greater the precision of the measure (Nunnally,
1967). For example, rather than asking a subject
to simply "agree" or "disagree" with a statement
(which yields only two response categories), it
is probably better to ask subjects to indicate
their opinions along a continuum of agreement,
perhaps as follows:

Strongly Disgree	Disagree	No Opinion	Agree	Strongly Agree
-2	-1	0	1	2

There are limits to subjects' abilities to
discriminate accurately, however. For example,

while subjects would have little difficulty
evaluating a statement in terms of the five categories presented above, a continuum which ranged
from one to 100 would encourage meaningless
distinctions. Thus, for any given measure, the
desire for fine distinctions must be weighed
against the likelihood of yielding accurate and
meaningful distinctions.

Both quantification and discriminability are
important factors in the assessment of measuring
instruments. If two measures were equally adequate in other ways, but one provided more easily
obtained quantitative data or more discriminating
data, this would be the more adequate measure.

4. Sensitivity to Change and Age Differences
In longitudinal studies of any kind, including
designs intended to evaluate the impact of service programs, it is imperative that the outcome
measure be sufficiently sensitive to detect
changes that occur. Unless the investigator
is confident that the outcome measure is sensitive to change, it cannot be determined whether
a lack of significant results reflects a true
lack of change or use of an instrument insensitive to the change that occurred.

A measure's sensitivity to change is exceedingly difficult to determine. Sensitivity to
change is in part an empirical phenomenon, but
it also has theoretical and research design
components. Theoretically, some phenomena are
expected to be more changeable than others.
For example, affect (e.g., happiness) is much
more changeable than a personality dimension
such as introversion-extraversion. It is also
imperative to choose an outcome variable

appropriate to the presumed causal agent. Thus,
a measure of self-perceived health may be an
appropriate outcome variable for an examination
of the impact of home health care services, but
far less appropriate as an outcome measure for
a study of the impact of improved transportation
services.

Characteristics of the sample can also affect
an instrument's sensitivity to change. Subjects
studied must be able to experience change in the
outcome variable. For example, if an investigator wishes to demonstrate the impact of home
health services upon perceived health, there must
be some initial evidence that the subjects are
capable of increasing their health perceptions.
If the researcher inadvertently obtains a sample
of subjects who largely view themselves as pos-
sessing excellent health, there is little room
for demonstrated improvement in self-perceived
health. This is conventionally called the problem of "ceiling effects." Similar problems can
occur at the lower end of an instrument's metric
and are called "floor effects."

In the study of social gerontology, it is
particularly important that instruments are sensitive to age differences. The issue of whether
an instrument is sensitive to age changes is
different than the issue of applicability to
older subjects. An instrument may be applicable
to and understood by subjects of varying ages
and still not be sufficiently sensitive to detect
age differences. Evidence for this sensitivity
must be largely empirical--either scores differ
significantly across age groups, or they do not.
However, the issue is complicated by potential
confounding factors. Observed age differences

may in fact result from other differences between groups--factors such as differences in health which are correlated with age. Well-developed and articulated theoretical expectations can help in the interpretation of age differences, but there may be associated difficulties. For example, in the case of some phenomena, it is not theoretically clear whether age differences should be expected.

In summary, it is difficult to assess an instrument's sensitivity to change or to age differences because (1) there is no direct test of sensitivity, and (2) non-measurement issues (i.e., theory, sampling, features of the research design) influence the instrument's sensitivity in the research situation.

5. <u>Reliability</u>. Reliability is a standard criterion used to assess the adequacy of measuring instruments. Reliability is most simply defined as the degree to which a measuring instrument is free of random error--the less the amount of random error, the greater the reliability and accuracy of the instrument (Bohrnstedt, 1969).

The consequences of using unreliable measures are profound. Unreliable measurement most frequently results in a lack of significant findings, since random error may confuse and mask underlying patterns. However, in certain unusual circumstances, unreliability will result in statistically significant, but misleading and inaccurate research findings.

A rather sophisticated body of psychometric theory provides the tools by which to calculate

reliability estimates. Specific formulae for
reliability coefficients will not be presented
in this document (for a thorough and cogent
review, see Nunnally, 1967). However, three
major approaches to reliability will be briefly
described.

Internal Consistency. Measures of internal
consistency may be used to estimate the reliability of multi-item scales. In this approach,
the items are correlated with each other in all
possible combinations and the sizes of the correlations are examined.

The set of intercorrelations between items is
used to calculate a reliability coefficient,
typically called alpha and symbolized as α (Cronbach, 1951). This reliability coefficient can
range in value from zero, which represents total
error (perfect unreliability), to one (perfect
reliability). The higher the value, the better
the reliability. Reliability coefficients of .90
or higher are considered very high, while coefficients of lower than .65 or so are considered
relatively unreliable and suggest that the measure
may pose a potential threat to the quality of the
study.

The logic behind internal consistency reliability estimates is relatively straightforward.
If the items are in fact all tapping the same
underlying construct, then they should be highly
intercorrelated. If the items are not highly
intercorrelated, either some of the items are
unreliable or the set of items is tapping more
than one underlying dimension.

Split-Half. Split-half reliability estimates,

like internal consistency reliability coefficients, can be calculated only on multi-item instruments. Using this approach, the instrument
is divided into two presumably equivalent forms.
Both forms are administered to individuals and
a correlation is calculated between scores on
the two forms. The correlation coefficient is
the reliability estimate. The higher the correlation, the higher the presumed reliability.

There are two potential problems with this
approach. First, the investigator can never be
sure that the two forms are actually equivalent.
Second, if the correlation is weak or moderate,
the investigator has no clues as to which half
is the more reliable or which items incorporate
the majority of random error.

Test-Retest. Using this approach, the instrument is administered twice to the same set of
individuals. A correlation is then calculated
between the two scores. The higher the correlation, the higher the presumed reliability.

There are serious threats to the accuracy of
test-retest reliability estimates. The general
issue is the possibility that an intervening experience may alter the individual's true score
on the measure of interest. The test-retest
correlation may consequently be lowered and the
true change (a property of the organism) interpreted as unreliability (a property of the instrument). A more specific example of this general issue is the case of practice effects. The
experience of taking a particular test or instrument may actually alter the individual's score
when the test is taken a second time. Another
specific example is the potential impact of

maturational effects--the possibility that some inherent growth or aging process will change the individual's performance on the measure. Practice effects or maturational effects are particular cases of the confounding of true change with unreliability.

In general, the longer the interval between the two tests, the less the likelihood of practice effects. Unfortunately, however the longer the interval between tests, the greater the likelihood of true change or maturational effects having an impact on the individual. Thus, there is no real solution to the potential problems with test-retest correlations. Good judgment and prudent interpretation must be used consistently.

Heise (1969) has suggested a modified test-retest approach for separating unreliability from true change over time. This method, however, requires at least three waves of longitudinal data and makes rather stringent assumptions about the nature of the variable being measured. Thus far, Heise's proposed method of reliability assessment has not been widely adopted.

It should be noted that test-retest correlation is the only possible method of reliability estimation that can be used with single-item measuring instruments. This highlights the limited adequacy of single-item, as compared to multi-item, instruments.

In spite of the fact that there exists no infallible method of assessing reliability, it is important that efforts be made to evaluate this critical characteristic of the instrument.

Reliability is clearly a criterion for which an admittedly limited assessment is far superior to no evaluation at all.

6.   <u>Validity</u>. Validity is probably the most important criterion in measurement development and assessment, and also the most difficult to evaluate. Validity may be defined as the degree to which a particular instrument measures the variable or phenomenon it is intended to measure (Nunnally, 1967). Reliability is a necessary component of validity, but does not, by itself, guarantee validity (Kerlinger, 1973; Selltiz, Wrightsman, and Cook, 1976). A measure may be perfectly reliable (i.e., contain no random error) and still not measure the intended phenomenon.

There is no direct and certain test of validity. Instead, assessment of validity must be conducted by a variety of indirect methods, each of which has limitations and potential threats to its accuracy. The three most commonly used approaches to the assessment of validity will be discussed briefly.

<u>Convergent</u> <u>Validity</u>. Convergent validity is based on the logic that instruments that measure the same variable should correlate highly (Campbell and Fiske, 1959). Using this approach, measures which are intended to tap the same underlying phenomenon are administered to the same set of individuals. The higher the correlations among measures, the greater the inferred validity. The limitation of this approach is that the validity of the other measures is also uncertain. Therefore, low correlations cannot inform the investigator which measure(s) is (are) not valid.

Discriminant Validity. This approach is virtually the converse of convergent validity. The logic of this approach is to determine whether the instrument can discriminate between the phenomenon it is intended to measure and different, but related phenomena (Campbell and Fiske, 1959). To the extent that an instrument exhibits this ability to discriminate, there is evidence of discriminant validity. Thus, the correlation between happiness and satisfaction might be expected to be moderate (i.e., theoretically a relationship between the two is expected), but not so high as to lose the distinction between the two constructs. As in the case of convergent validity, to the degree that the correlations between measures are not of the expected magnitude, it is not clear which measure(s) is(are) not sufficiently discriminating, or whether the theoretical expectations about the degree of expected relationship were inaccurate.

Predictive Validity. If an instrument is valid, it should predict other variables in a manner and to a degree compatible with theoretical expectations (Nunnally, 1967). For example, if high school grades constitute a valid measure of academic promise, we might expect high school grades to predict academic performance in college. This is an empirical proposition that can be tested. Although the term predictive conventionally connotes a future orientation, predictive validity procedures refer to a predicted relationship between distinct concepts, regardless of the temporal issues involved. In some cases, predictive validity assessment will require longitudinal measurement; in other cases, concurrent measurement is appropriate.

One specific predictive validity strategy merits attention. In some cases it is possible to assess predictive validity using known groups or criterion groups analysis. The logic of this approach is to determine whether groups that theoretically would be expected to score differently on a particular measure in fact do score differently. For example, let's assume that we have developed a scale for measuring clinical depression. If (1) we administer our scale to a group of persons diagnosed as having clinical depression and to a group of individuals who are not suffering from depression and (2) the instrument significantly discriminates between the two groups, we have evidence supporting the validity of our scale. In cases where meaningful criterion groups can be identified and compared, known groups analysis can be an effective method of testing predictive validity.

Thus, to the extent that a measure predicts other variables in a theoretically meaningful manner, there is evidence of predictive validity. The interpretation of negative results is, unfortunately, less straightforward: invalidity of the instrument cannot be distinguished from erroneous theory.

While it is difficult to establish the validity of any particular measure, it is a sufficiently important criterion that the indirect methods of evaluation available are well worth examining. The best instruments are those for which evidence of convergent, discriminant, and predictive validity is available. In spite of the fact that all the methods are indirect, evidence from a combination of methods is persuasive.

7.   Scalability. Multi-item measures intended
to tap one underlying phenomenon must be examined
for scalability. First, the scale must be mathe-
matically unidimensional or comprise a known and
specified number of dimensions (Bohrnstedt, 1969).
Second, each of the items in the scale should
significantly contribute to the scale as a whole
(Selltiz, Wrightsman, and Cook, 1976). Finally,
the relative contribution of each item in the
scale should be known and specified (Selltiz,
Wrightsman, and Cook, 1976). This is typically
demonstrated in a weighting procedure, where the
different weights assigned to the items reflect
the differential contributions of individual
items. A relatively complex body of psychometric
theory guides the assessment of scalability; for
an excellent review, the reader is referred to
Nunnally (1967).

It should be noted that the need to satisfy
an additional criterion does not mean that it is
more difficult to assess the adequacy of scales
than other types of instruments. In fact, scales
have certain advantages in this regard (i.e.,
it is easier to estimate and increase the reliability of a scale than of a single-item measure).
At any rate, all well-established and standard
scales should have available information about
the scalar properties noted above.

COMPARABILITY OF RESEARCH RESULTS

Once the adequacy of a measuring instrument
is established, continued use of that instrument
is encouraged. It makes little sense to develop
a new measure--to "reinvent the wheel" in effect--
when an adequate one already exists. More

importantly, the use of standardized, frequently-used instruments permits comparison of results across studies. The growth of comparable research results permits generalization to broader segments of the population and a refinement of observed patterns, contributing to the cumulative nature of scientific evidence.

SUMMARY

This chapter has noted the conventional criteria used to assess the adequacy of measuring instruments in the social sciences. The seven criteria reviewed are adequacy of samples, establishment of normative values, discriminability and quantification, sensitivity to change and age differences, reliability, validity, and scalability. These criteria will be used to assess the instruments reviewed in subsequent chapters. The applicability of the measuring instruments to older samples also will be highlighted.

Chapter 3

LIFE SATISFACTION AND RELATED CONCEPTS

CONCEPTUAL ISSUES

In spite of the materialistic striving typical
of this society, or, perhaps because of the relative affluence such striving has generated, Americans devote considerable attention to their inner
selves. The Declaration of Independence proclaims
"the pursuit of happiness" one of the inalienable
rights of all people. Thus, from the beginning,
our society has viewed a subjective sense of well-
being as an important personal and social goal.

Two broad bodies of research inform social
science perspectives on life satisfaction. First,
social epidemiological studies of the incidence
and prevalence of mental illness in the American
population have suggested a variety of measures
of life satisfaction and have related life satisfaction to mental health (c.f., Gurin, Veroff,
and Feld, 1960; Bradburn, 1969). Specific studies
which use life satisfaction as a measure of life

37

quality (Campbell, Converse and Rodgers, 1976;
Andrews and Withey, 1976) are a recent direct
outgrowth of this research. Second, several
studies in social gerontology have used measures of life satisfaction as indicators of
adjustment in late life (c.f., Cumming and
Henry, 1961; Lemon, Bengtson, and Peterson,
1972). A number of related concepts have
emerged from these research domains, all of
which are presumed to reflect a general sense
of well-being. In many instances, the terms
"life satisfaction," "morale," and "happiness"
are used interchangeably. In fact, however,
the use of sloppy semantics leads to confusion
and blurs significant conceptual distinctions.

In conventional usage, "satisfaction" refers
to the fulfillment of needs, expectations,
wishes, or desires (Webster, 1968). Life
satisfaction refers to an assessment of the
overall conditions of existence as derived
from a comparison of one's aspirations to
one's actual achievements (Cantril, 1965;
Campbell, Converse, and Rodgers, 1976). A
report of life satisfaction is essentially
a cognitive assessment of one's progress
toward desired goals (Andrews and Withey,
1976). Further, in that "life as a whole"
or "life in general" is the referent, a long-
range time perspective (Campbell, Converse,
and Rodgers, 1976) and non-specific life
conditions (Andrews and Withey, 1976) are
implied.

In social gerontology, the concept of life
satisfaction has had a wide and varied usage,
typically with less conceptual clarity than
in the definitions presented above. For example,

Neugarten (1974) views life satisfaction for older people as the extent to which the individual:

1) takes pleasure from whatever round of activities that constitute his everyday life;

2) regards his life as meaningful and accepts responsibility for what his life has been;

3) feels he has succeeded in achieving his major life goals;

4) holds a positive self-image and regards himself as a worthwhile person, no matter what his present weaknessess may be; and

5) maintains optimistic attitudes and moods. (p. 13)

Although Neugarten's definition does include the degree to which desired goals have been achieved, it also includes factors which less obviously reflect life satisfaction per se. In particular, the definition appears to include a self-esteem component. This definition, while incorporating several components of life experience, appears to go beyond the definition of life satisfaction and is conceptually ambiguous.

Sociologists have traditionally used the term morale to describe feelings of esprit de corps or a sense of meaningful integration into a social group. Thus, morale has been viewed as a characteristic of groups or of individuals.

Morale is defined in the dictionary as one's "mental condition with respect to courage, discipline, confidence, enthusiasm, and willingness to endure hardship" (Webster, 1968). Perhaps because old age is conceptualized as a life stage fraught with potential adversity, gerontologists frequently discuss the well-being of older people in terms of morale (c.f., Streib, 1956; Maddox, 1963; Bultena, 1969), and occasionally refer specifically to "age-related morale" (Lawton, 1977). As initially used in the study of late life, morale was conceptualized as a mental state or set of dispositions which condition the individual's responses to problems of living (Kutner, Fanshel, Togo, and Langner, 1956). Lawton, the originator of a widely used morale measure, conceives of high morale as:

> a basic sense of satisfaction with oneself—
> a feeling that there is a place in the
> environment for oneself—that people and
> things in one's life offer some satisfac-
> tion to the individual—a fit between
> personal needs and what the environment
> offers . . . (and) a certain acceptance
> of what cannot be changed. (1976, p. 148)

Kutner, Fanshel, Togo, and Langner (1956) define morale as the presence or absence of "satisfaction, optimism, and expanding life perspectives." Thus, as used by social gerontologists, morale and life satisfaction possess some common qualities—a cognitive connotation and an orientation to life as a whole. Both Kutner et al. and Lawton, however, move beyond satisfaction to include other factors such as self-acceptance and optimism. These disparate factors make precise definitions of morale difficult.

Although sometimes used as a synonym for life satisfaction, happiness more precisely refers to transitory moods of gaiety or pleasure (Campbell, Converse, and Rodgers, 1976). Thus, happiness reflects the affect people feel toward their current state of affairs. In social science research, Bradburn provides the most frequently used conceptualization of happiness. He defines happiness as the extent to which positive feelings outweigh negative feelings, using the time referent of "the past few weeks" (1969).

Despite different time references and nuances of affect or cognition, life satisfaction, morale and happiness are all global concepts. Each refers to life as a whole rather than to specific domains of life experience. Because of their global nature, these concepts may have only limited utility in evaluation research. Carp (1977) cautions against drawing policy-relevant inferences from data which do not reveal why and with what people are satisfied. Domain-specific measures of satisfaction are an alternative approach to the use of global measures (Campbell, Converse, and Rodgers, 1976; Andrews and Withey, 1976). Such measures may constitute more appropriate criterion measures for specific evaluation studies. To evaluate the impact of residential relocation, for example, Carp (1975) developed a measure of "housing satisfaction" which may have a more direct and interpretable relationship to the effects of relocation than do global assessments of well-being.

Global and domain-specific measures are appropriate for different research questions. There is substantial evidence that global measures of life satisfaction are related to mental well-being (Andrews and Withey, 1976; Bradburn, 1969). If popularity is any indication of the usefulness of a concept, life satisfaction would be clearly indispensible, for gerontologists persistently use it as a criterion for successful aging. The appropriateness of life satisfaction as a concept and the choice of a global or domain-specific measurement approach should be guided by theoretical considerations.

Although it has been demonstrated that happiness is a transitory affective state, the stability of life satisfaction and morale is both conceptually and empirically problematic--a situation with both basic science and policy implications. It is unclear to what extent the concepts life satisfaction and morale should be viewed as relatively stable personality dimensions, as modifiable coping capacities, or as reactive products of manipulable objective conditions. Theoretical paradigms that should lend guidance are not sufficiently well articulated to do so. Thus, it is unclear under what conditions changes should be expected, and hence interpretation of empirical results is ambiguous.

If life satisfaction is a stable personality trait, it should be impervious to interventions, and hence an unsuitable criterion for program evaluation. If, on the other hand, life satisfaction is responsive to change in external conditions, two tasks remain before the effects of intervention on life satisfaction can be clearly discerned. First, norms as to the changes of life satisfaction across the life course should be established. Second, the conditions with which it varies should be cataloged.

Rosow (1977) has questioned the use of life satisfaction at all, inquiring about its scientific merit and its appropriateness as a criterion for policy planning. Subjective well-being is a useful scientific concept to the degree that explanation and understanding of it informs sociological theory. Subjective well-being is an attractive goal in public policy to the degree that our society has the technology to foster it and the public support to implement that technology. The demonstrated relative stability of life satisfaction (Andrews and Withey, 1976), as well as its link to achievement of serious and desired goals probably makes it a more attractive measure of subjective life quality to the research investigator than the more emotional and transitory reports of happiness. Life satisfaction also is typically a more appealing concept than happiness to policy and social service professionals (although not perhaps in studies of specific interventions). In the context of social policy, moderate levels of life satisfaction may be a more reasonable social objective than happiness.

METHODOLOGICAL ISSUES

The measurement of life satisfaction and related concepts involves a number of methodological considerations other than the criteria for evaluating instruments noted in Chapter Four. Three of these will be discussed briefly.

Theoretical Appropriateness of Particular Concepts/Measures

The concepts of life satisfaction, morale, and happiness have different meanings in terms of

affect versus cognition, transitory versus relative stability, long versus short term time
referent, and underlying conceptual framework.
Choice of a measure should reflect theoretical
decisions concerning the desired configuration of
these dimensions. The research question and its
theoretical foundation also should be used to
decide between global and domain-specific measures. All of these issues have been discussed
previously. They are reiterated here because
the choice of appropriate measuring instruments
must balance knowledge about the properties of
instruments against theoretical considerations
about the assumptions used to develop that instrument. It is in this sense that theory and
methodology, while analytically separable for
purposes of discussion, are necessarily inter-
twined in the research enterprise.

   Measures of life satisfaction and related concepts also differ in terms of their dimensionality.
Some measures are unidimensional (e.g., the
Cantril Ladder), while others are multi-dimensional (e.g., the Affect Balance Scale). In many
cases, although this is not true of the Affect
Balance Scale, these dimensions are empirically
rather than theoretically derived. The investigator should consider the implications of using
a multi-dimensional measure. It may be that some
variables under study will correlate highly with
some dimensions of the measure, but not with
others. Thus, the use of scores summed across
all items could result in information loss.

The Appropriateness of Particular Measures to Specific Samples

Life satisfaction measures are common in two

research traditions--social epidemiology and
social gerontology, as noted earlier. A number
of the measures developed in social surveys have
been inadequately standardized on samples of
older subjects. Some of the measures from the
field of social gerontology have not been administered to younger subjects, or have been inadequately standardized on younger samples. Several
of these measures have age-related question
content, and the suitability of these measures
to younger subjects is unclear. Interestingly,
however, the Life Satisfaction Index (Neugarten,
Havighurst and Tobin, 1961), previously administered only to older subjects, was recently used
in a Harris poll of the general adult population
(Louis Harris and Associates, 1975). It is important to keep in mind that all measures will
not be equally applicable to particular samples.

Subjective versus Objective Definition. Measures
of life satisfaction and related concepts are,
to some extent, caught in an unresolvable paradox.
The investigator typically seeks standardized
instruments in order to present the same "stimulus"
to all respondents and to gather comparable data
across subjects. Life satisfaction, morale, and
happiness all include an inherent component of
subjectivity, however, and the frames of reference
used by subjects to determine their self-assess-
ments differ widely across individuals. Thus,
if the investigator chooses particular items,
comparability is maximized while the salience of
the items to subjects' frames of references is
unknown but undoubtedly varies widely. In the
case of measures where subjects provide their
own definitions and frames of reference, the
converse is true. There is no apparent method of
maximizing both comparability across subjects and

salience to all subjects.

Measures have been developed, however, to maximize each of these components. Most measures of satisfaction-related concepts maximize comparability across subjects--the originators chose sets of items they felt would best tap satisfaction as they conceptualized it (e.g., Life Satisfaction Index, Affect Balance Scale). Some of the items in these measures permit respondents to make comparative assessments (e.g., to their earlier lives), but subjects are left little room for explicating links between their life conditions and their subjective experiences of life. A few measures do permit subjects to provide referents for their assessments. The Cantril Ladder (Kilpatrick and Cantril, 1960; Cantril, 1965), for example, is a self-anchoring scale in which subjects define the best possible life and the worst possible life for them. These definitions are used to represent the top and bottom of a ladder. Subjects also report their life satisfaction by noting the rung of the ladder that best represents their current life experiences.

The choice between a subject-defined versus an investigator-determined instrument again must be dictated by the research question under investigation.

INSTRUMENTS TO BE REVIEWED

In this chapter, we present five selected instruments which measure life satisfaction or related concepts. The Kutner Morale Scale (Kutner et al., 1956) is included primarily because it

was the forerunner of later life satisfaction and
morale instruments and is still frequently cited
in the gerontological literature. The Life Satisfaction Index (Neugarten, Havighurst, and Tobin,
1961) represents a landmark effort to measure
life satisfaction and is probably the most widely
used instrument for assessing subjective perceptions of well-being among older individuals. The
Cantril Ladder (Kilpartick and Cantril, 1960) is
included as an example of a less obtrusive strategy for discerning subjective perceptions of life
satisfaction and the conditions used by subjects
to make their assessments. The Philadelphia
Geriatric Center Morale Scale (Lawton, 1972) is
included because it represents the most technic-
ally sophisticated instrument currently available
and because it has been administered to institutionalized older samples. Finally, the Affect
Balance Scale (Bradburn, 1969) is included because it is a measure of affect, because it has
been widely used in studies of well-being among
people of all ages, and because its psychometric
properties have been well described.

MORALE SCALE

(Kutner, Fanshel, Togo and Langner, 1956)

Description of Instrument

According to the authors, morale is a mental
state or set of dispositions which condition
one's response to problems of living. The Morale
Scale consists of seven items, five of which are
open-ended. A respondent's score is determined
by the number of affirmative responses given to
items which suggest high morale, as defined by
the authors. The measure is intended for interview administration. According to the authors,
the instrument was designed to form a Guttman
scale.

The instrument is generally believed to be
unidimensional and to reflect an unspecified but
long-term time referent (Cumming, Dean and Newell,
1958).

Research Content and Use

Kutner et al. (1956) developed this morale
measure as an indicator of adjustment and used
it in a survey of the needs of older residents
(age 60+) in a New York health district. The
sample consisted of 500 older people, a majority
from lower and middle socioeconomic groups, with
a mean educational attainment of grade school
completion.

Cumming, Dean, and Newell (1958) administered
four items from the Kutner measure in conjunction

with three items from the Srole Anomie Scale.

Simpson, Back, and McKinney (1966) and Kerckhoff (1966) used the Morale Scale in a study of 304 retired workers and 161 workers close to retirement in North Carolina. Norms are not reported.

Although rarely used in its original form, this instrument has served as a point of departure for later instrument development.

Measurement Properties

Reliability. Simpson, Back, and McKinney (1966) report that the Morale Scale has a Guttman scale reproducibility coefficient of .94. Lawton (1977) criticizes the Morale Scale in terms of its brevity, noting that measures with very few items are unlikely to meet acceptable reliability standards.

Validity. Evidence concerning the validity of the Morale Scale is quite limited. Cumming, Dean, and Newell (1958) report that the instrument they used did not correlate well with their choice of an external criterion: the judgment of an observer. There are two difficulties with this, however. First, Cumming et al. used only four of the seven items. Second, it is difficult to justify the use of an external rater as an appropriate criterion for the validity of a subjective state.

Sensitivity to Change. There is no evidence on the sensitivity of the Morale Scale to change.

Appropriateness for Older Samples. To our

knowledge, the Morale Scale has been administered only to samples of older people.

Comments and Recommendations

Because the instrument consists of items later incorporated into other more sophisticated and well-documented instruments, use of the Morale Scale is not recommended except in exploratory studies. The open-ended questions do make it a potentially useful tool for such initial work, however. The primary significance of this measure is its historical importance in the study of social gerontology.

Essential Reference

Kutner, B., Fanshel, D., Togo, A.M., and Langner, T.S. Five Hundred Over Sixty: A Community in Aging. New York: Russell Sage Foundation, 1956.

LIFE. SATISFACTION INDEX-A

(Neugarten, Havighurst and Tobin, 1961)

LIFE SATISFACTION INDEX-Z

(Wood, Wylie and Sheafer, 1969)

Description of Instrument

Neugarten, Havighurst and Tobin (1961) con-
ceive of life satisfaction as a construct which
encompasses five underlying dimensions of psychological well-being: zest, resolution and forti-
tude, congruence between desired and achieved
goals, positive self-concept and mood tone. The
Life Satisfaction Index-A (LSI-A) as developed
by Neugarten, Havighurst and Tobin consists of
twenty statements with which subjects agree or
disagree. Items utilize a long-term time referent.

According to the originators, the LSI-A is
multidimensional. Using factor analysis, Adams
(1969) found four clearly discernable factors:
mood tone, zest for life, congruence between
achieved and desired goals, and a fourth, unnamed
dimension. Bigot (1974) further explores the
underlying dimensions of the LSI-A.

The Life Satisfaction Index-Z (LSI-Z) is a
modification of the LSI-A developed by Wood,
Wylie and Sheafer (1969). It consists of 13
items drawn from the LSI-A.

Research Context and Use

Neugarten, Havighurst and Tobin (1961) devel-
loped the LSI-A in the context of the Kansas City
Studies of Adult Life. The investigators wished
to improve upon life satisfaction ratings given
by clinicians, and attempted to develop a standardized, valid and multidimensional measure of
well-being. The resulting LSI-A was standardized
on a sample of 92 noninstitutionalized people
aged 50-90 from middle and working class urban
backgrounds. The potential range of the measure
is 0-20. In the original sample, the mean score
was 12.4 with a standard deviation of 4.4.

Bigot (1974) administered the instrument to
150 British males aged 55-79 in manual and professional occupations. The wording of the items
was changed slightly for British respondents.
The mean life satisfaction score was 14.1 with a
standard deviation of 3.33.

Wood, Wylie and Sheafer (1969) surveyed 281
elderly residents of a rural Kansas community.
The mean life satisfaction score was 11.6 with
a standard deviation of 4.4.

Adams (1969) surveyed 508 elderly adults in
small midwestern towns and found the mean life
satisfaction score to be 12.5 with a standard
deviation of 3.6.

An 18-item version of the LSI was administered
to 4,254 respondents in a national sample (Louis
Harris and Associates, 1975). The sample was a
cross-section of the American public (aged 18+),
with substantial oversampling of older persons
and blacks. This is the first known study in

which the LSI was administered to younger subjects. The results indicate that on only seven
items did younger subjects exhibit substantially
higher life satisfaction than older subjects.

The LSI-Z was the end product of refinement
procedures by Wood, Wylie and Sheafer (1969).
Items on the LSI-A which did not highly correlate
with the instrument as a whole were eliminated.
The LSI-Z was standardized on 100 older persons
from rural Kansas. No norms were reported for
this group.

Wylie (1970) examined the usefulness of life
satisfaction as a program impact criterion.
Using 131 elderly subjects from the Wood, Wylie
and Sheafer (1969) study, Wylie attempted to
determine the impact of participation in a volunteer service program on the morale of older
people. Wylie found morale to increase from
18.92 to 20.65 among the participants in the
program and to decrease from 18.58 to 16.42
during the same time period for the non-partici-
pants.

Measurement Properties

Reliability. No reliability estimates are
reported for the LSI-A. For the LSI-Z, however,
Wood, Wylie and Sheafer (1969) report a split-
half reliability coefficient of .79.

Validity. Neugarten, Havighurst and Tobin
(1969) report a correlation of .55 between the
LSI-A and the clinically-based Life Satisfaction
Ratings instrument. Similarly, Wood, Wylie and
Sheafer report a correlation of .57 between the
LSI-Z and the Life Satisfaction Ratings

instrument. These correlations are weak evidence of the convergent validity of the LSI-A and LSI-Z since both instruments originated from the Life Satisfaction Ratings instrument.

In a study of older Chicagoans, Bild and Havighurst (1976) report that an 18-item version of the LSI-A has a .66 correlation with the Affect Balance Scale.

Lohmann (1977), in a study of 259 older people in Knoxville, Tennessee, found that the LSI-A correlated .76 with the Philadelphia Geriatric Center Morale Scale and, not surprisingly, .94 with its offspring, the LSI-A. She also reports a correlation of .79 between the LSI-Z and the Philadelphia Geriatric Center Morale Scale.

Sensitivity to Change. In the Wylie (1970) study, life satisfaction (measured pre- and post-intervention) significantly increased for participants in a community program. As she notes, "The LSI-Z demonstrated its capacity to record positive and negative change--an important criterion for an evaluation tool" (p. 39).

Appropriateness for Older Samples. Both the LSI-A and LSI-Z were developed for use on older samples. The survey by Louis Harris and Associates (1975) suggests that the LSI-A is appropriate for all adults. Consequently, the LSI-A appears useful for the study of age differences in life satisfaction.

Comments and Recommendations

The original LSI-A consists of 20 items, although an 18-item version also is in use (see

Adams, 1969; Louis Harris and Associates, 1975;
Bild and Havighurst, 1976). Similarly, the
original LSI-Z (which is a subset of the LSI-A)
consists of 13 items, while a 10-item version
also is in use (see Edwards and Klemmack, 1974).
For each version, there are several alternative
scoring procedures. It should be noted that
comparison of results across published studies
should be done carefully, making sure that the
comparisons made refer to the same instrument
and scoring method.

It is important to note that the Life Satisfaction Indexes are multidimensional instruments
and that they contain more than a sense of congruence between aspirations and achievements (our
preferred definition of life satisfaction). Knapp
(1976) suggests that, in light of its demonstrated
multidimensionality, the LSI-A should be used as
a series of subscales, each representing a separate dimension. He claims that using the instrument as if a single score represents a single
dimension blurs the relationships between the
underlying discrete dimensions and independent
variables, including age. We support Knapp's
recommendation.

Nonetheless, both the LSI-A and LSI-Z are
convenient, easily administered measures which
rest upon a substantial amount of empirical
support.

Essential References

Neugarten, B.L., Havighurst, R.J., and Tobin, S.S.
    The Measurement of Life Satisfaction. Journal
    of Gerontology, 1961, 16, 134-143.

This classic article details the early development of the LSI-A and presents the instrument in standard form.

Wood, V., Wylie, M.L., and Sheafer, B. An Analysis of a Short Self-Report Measure of Life Satisfaction: Correlation with Rater Judgments. Journal of Gerontology, 1969, 24, 465-469.

This article describes the development of the LSI-Z and presents the instrument in standard form.

SELF-ANCHORING SCALE

(Cantril, 1965)

Description of Instrument

Cantril (1965) conceives of life satisfaction
as the extent to which people's perceptions of
their current lives coincide with their definitions of the best possible life. The instrument
asks respondents to rate their present lives in
relation to their perceptions of the worst possible and best possible lives. Respondents are
shown a picture of a ladder with ten or eleven
numbered rungs. The top rung represents the best
possible life (as the subject defines it) and
the bottom rung represents the worst possible
life (as the subject defines it). The respondent
also points out the rung that represents his or
her current situation. The individual's score
is simply the number of the rung to which he
points.

The instrument is a single-item measure of
global life satisfaction with an emphasis upon
life in the present. As developed by Cantril
the ladder rating is to be elicited by an interviewer who probes responses to determine the
respondent's substantive aspirations.

Research Context and Use

This self-anchoring technique was developed
to offer respondents the opportunity to define
in their own terms the anchor points of any
dimension to be measured (Kilpatrick and Cantril,

1960). This technique may be applied to a variety
of objects or situations (Campbell, Converse, and
Rodgers, 1976), but Cantril (1965), in his cross-
cultural research, focused upon people's perceptions of best and worst lives, their own satisfaction, and the hopes and fears they held with
respect to the future of their nations. In the
1965 study, Cantril surveyed over 20,000 persons
around the world, including 1,549 Americans drawn
from a national probability sample.

Cantril reports that in 1959 the mean in life
satisfaction as measured by ladder rating for the
U.S. sample was 6.6. For respondents age 21-29,
the mean was 6.3; for those 30-49, the mean was
6.5; for those 50-64, the mean was 6.8; and for
people 65 and over, the mean was 6.5. For whites,
the mean rating was 6.7, and for non-whites, 5.3.
For people of upper socioeconomic status, the
mean score was 7.1; for those of middle status,
6.6; and for those people in the lowest socioeconomic category, 6.0.

The Cantril Ladder has been used specifically
as a measure of life satisfaction related to late
life in the studies of Bortner and Hultsch (1970),
Palmore and Luikart (1972) and Palmore and Kivett
(1977). The merits and deficiences of this measurement approach have been further examined by
Campbell, Converse, and Rodgers (1976) and
Andrews and Withey (1976).

In a multivariate secondary analysis of the
1965 Cantril data, Bortner and Hultsch examined
the records of 1,406 subjects from the national
probability sample. Using an 11-rung ladder
(rungs numbered 0-10), the mean life satisfaction
score was 7.64 and the standard deviation 2.05.

Palmore and Kivett (1977) studied life satisfaction longitudinally by examining three waves of data in the Duke Longitudinal Study II, collected at two year intervals. The mean life satisfaction score at round one was 7.1; at round two, 7.2; and at round three, 7.0.

Andrews and Withey (1976) performed a methodological study of 68 measures of subjective well-being--including the Cantril Ladder. Using a nine-rung ladder, these authors examined distributions of life satisfaction for 1,433 respondents in a national survey. For respondents age 15-19, the mean was 6.4; for those 20-24 and 25-29, the mean was 6.0; for those 30-34, the mean was 6.1; for people 35-44 and 45-54, the mean was 6.0; for those 55-64, the mean was 6.1; and for people 65 and over, the mean was 6.2 (Andrews and Withey, 1976, p. 323).

Measurement Properties

Reliability. Palmore and Kivett (1977) report a test-retest reliability coeffiecient of .65 over a two-year interval.

Validity. Cantril demonstrated that average ratings of life satisfaction, calculated on a national basis, are correlated with a variety of social structural factors including racial composition, national per capita income, and national educational levels. This is at best weak evidence of predictive validity.

Similarly, Palmore and Kivett (1977) report that the validity of the Cantril Ladder as a measure of life satisfaction "is demonstrated by its significant correlations with variables with which it theoretically should be correlated" (p. 312). These correlates include levels of social activity, self-ratings of health and income. Again this is rather weak evidence of validity.

Andrews and Withey (1976) report the strongest available evidence of the convergent validity of the Cantril Ladder. Correlations between Cantril Ladder life satisfaction ratings and fourteen other measures of subjective well-being range from .00 to .68. Its correlations with what these authors demonstrate to be the most valid measures, however, range from .46 to .49.

Sensitivity to Change. There is not a direct test of the sensitivity of Cantril Ladder ratings to change. The longitudinal findings reported by Palmore and Kivett over a four-year interval, indicate little change over that time. On the other hand, it might be that the subjects' life conditions remained very stable.

Appropriateness for Older Samples. The Cantril Ladder has been administered to adults of all ages and evidently poses no problems.

Comments and Recommendations

The Cantril Ladder measurement technique has one distinct advantage in that it permits individuals to describe and evaluate their lives in terms of their own perceptions and values.

Significantly more information concerning the instrument's reliability is needed in order to use the measure with confidence. Further, Andrews and Withey (1976) suggest that the unlabeled response categories are problematic.

Nonetheless, this is a relatively unique approach to the measurement of life satisfaction and merits further refinement and consideration.

It should be noted that there are nine-rung, ten-rung, and eleven-rung Cantril Ladder instruments in use. Therefore, caution is urged in comparing results across studies.

Essential References

Cantril, H. The Pattern of Human Concerns. New Burnswick, New Jersey: Rutgers University Press, 1965.

This volume details Cantril's cross-cultural survey of satisfactions and aspirations. Investigators will find this volume useful in describing the uses and purposes of the Cantril Ladder technique. This reference also contains the instrument in standard form.

Andrews, F.M., and Withey, S.B. Social Indicators of Well-Being. New York: Plenum Press, 1976.

This book presents a detailed and sophisticated examination of the measurement properties of 68 measures of subjective well-being--including the Cantril Ladder life satisfaction measure.

PHILADELPHIA GERIATRIC CENTER MORALE SCALE

(Lawton, 1972)

Description of Instrument

To Lawton, morale consists of positive self-regard, a struggle for mastery and acceptance of reality.

As developed by Lawton (1972), the Philadelphia Geriatric Center (PGC) Morale Scale has 22 items which the respondent is asked to agree or disagree with, or, for a few items, to choose among other dichotomous response alternatives. The instrument may be administered in either paper-and-pencil or interviewer format. One point is scored for each response exhibiting high morale. The instrument utilizes a long-term referent.

According to Lawton (1972), the instrument was constructed to be multidimensional. Using factor analysis, six factors were discovered: surgency, attitudes toward own aging, agitation, acceptance of the status quo, optimism, and lonely dissatisfaction.

After examination of the factor structure on several later samples, Lawton (1975) revised the PGC Morale Scale, dropping five items. Three dimensions are included in the 17-item measure: agitation, attitudes toward own aging, and lonely dissatisfaction.

Research Context and Use

This instrument was designed to fill the void
of measures appropriate for use with very old,
institutionalized subjects. It was constructed
to prevent respondent confusion or fatigue by
reducing the complexity of the items and response
categories. Lawton attempted to construct a
measure long enough to foster reliability, but
short enough that it would not tire the respondent.

The instrument was administered in its original form to two samples; the first was 208
tenants of the Philadelphia Geriatric Center,
mean age of 77.9. The second sample consisted
of 172 residents of a Lutheran home for the aged,
mean age of 78.8. Normative data are not
reported.

A number of studies have employed the PGC
instrument, but few mention normative data. The
primary task in these studies has been the de-
lineation of the factor structure, rather than
providing normative values or relating the instrument to other variables.

Morris and Sherwood (1975) administered the
PGC Morale Scale to two samples of older persons:
applicants to a long-term care facility and applicants to a low income public housing project.
No normative data were presented. The authors
concur with Lawton's 1975 revision, suggesting
a three-factor, 17-item version of the PGC
Morale Scale.

Using a 16-item modified version of the
PGC, Morris (1975) examined the morale of 209

applicants to the Hebrew Rehabilitation Center
for the Aged in Boston over a twelve month interval.   Again, no descriptive data are reported.
This 16-item version of the PGC Morale Scale
also is known as the Hebrew Rehabilitation Center Life Satisfaction Scale.

In a study of the effects of social interaction among residents at a home for the aged
in Pittsburgh, Kalson (1976) compared the
morale of 17 people aged 61-96 with 16 non-
participants before and after participation
in group interaction with retarded adults.
Among the participants in the experiment,
morale increased from 11.23 to 14.38.   In
the control group, morale increased from 12.31
to 13.15.

Measurement Properties

Reliability.   Lawton (1972) reports a split-
half reliability coefficient of .74, a coefficient
of internal consistency of .81, and test-retest
reliability coefficients ranging from .75
to .91.

Validity.   Lawton (1972) correlated scores
on the PGC Morale Scale with ratings of institutionalized patients' morale levels.   The
raters were professionals employed by the
institution and were given a definition of
morale based on Lawton's conceptualization.
The correlation between the PGC Morale Scale
and the ratings was .47.   Lawton also reports
that the PGC Morale Scale and the Neugarten,
Havighurst, and Tobin Life Satisfaction Ratings
(the clinician ratings instrument) correlated
at the .57 level.

Lohmann (1977), in a study of 259 older people in Tennessee, found that the correlation between the PGC Morale Scale and the LSI-A is .76, while the correlation between the PGC Morale Scale and the LSI-Z is .79.

Sensitivity to Change. There is limited evidence supporting sensitivity to change. Kalson (1976) reports that compared to controls, subjects who participated in a volunteer program experienced increases in morale.

Morris (1975) used a 16-item subset of the PGC Morale Scale to measure applicants to a long-term care center at two points in time, one year apart. Some items changed more over this twelve month period than others.

Appropriateness for Older Samples. This instrument was developed for use with older samples.

Comments and Recommendations

This instrument is easily administered and is applicable to normal older adults as well as impaired and institutionalized ones. In light of the recommendations of Lawton (1975) and Morris and Sherwood (1975), the 17-item version of the PGC Morale Scale is recommended.

While more information about the reliability and validity of the PGC Morale Scale would be useful, the factor structure of the measure is well delineated. In this light, the investigator should note that this is a multidimensional instrument. Not all of the subscales directly related to satisfaction with one's achievements toward desired goals. Thus, interpretation must be carefully made and might best be reported in factor-specific terms.

Essential References

Lawton, M.P. The Dimensions of Morale. In D.
 Kent, R. Kastenbaum, and S. Sherwood (Eds.),
 Research, Planning and Action for the Elderly.
 New York: Behavioral Publications, 1972.

In this chapter, Lawton explains the purposes of the Morale Scale and presents the instrument in standard form.

Lawton, M.P. The Philadelphia Geriatric Center
 Morale Scale: A Revision. Journal of Gerontology, 1975, 30, 85-89.

In this article, Lawton describes the revision of the PGC Morale Scale and describes the factor structure in detail.

AFFECT BALANCE SCALE

(Bradburn, 1969)

Description of Instrument

In Bradburn's formulation, happiness is the degree to which a person's positive feelings about his life outweigh his negative feelings. The Affect Balance Scale (ABS) is a ten-item measure of global feelings toward life in the present. The items ask people whether they have experienced ten specific feelings (five positive, five negative) in the past few weeks. Respondents need only answer yes or no to the questions.

Research Context and Use

As developed in an early form by Bradburn and Caplovitz in 1965, the ABS was intended as an indicator of mental health in surveys of large samples. It was hoped that time series data would be collected, using the instrument to relate psychological states to major social changes.

Bradburn (1969) defines happiness as the degree to which positive affect toward life as it has unfolded during the few weeks prior to the interview exceeds negative affect. Positive and negative affect are assumed to be independent; thus, a decline in positive feelings would not necessarily be accompanied by an increase in negative feelings. Empirically, the items of the ABS do in fact form separate negative and positive dimensions.

The instrument was standardized using five broad samples, heterogeneous with respect to race, social class, occupation and urban versus rural residence.   The age range of these approximately 2,800 respondents was 18 to 60 years. Scores on the ABS range from -4 to +4, with positive scores representing greater degree of happiness.   The frequency distribution of scores among the respondents can be found in Bradburn (1969, p. 66).

The ABS has been adopted for use in several studies of older adults despite the absence of older subjects in Bradburn's samples.

Gaitz and Scott (1972) administered the ABS as part of a study to determine the relationships between age and various measures of mental well-being.   The sample consisted of 1,441 noninstitutionalized adults from Houston's three major ethnic groups--Anglo, Black and Mexican-American. Respondents ranged in age from 20 to 75+ years. The sample included equal proportions of men and women and high and low occupational skills in each of the age and ethnic groups.   The investigators determined that the ABS had no significant relationship with age.   The scores of the older respondents covered the full range (scored 0-10 in this study) with about 2/3 of the scores falling in the 5 to 8 interval.

Beiser (1974) studied the mental well-being of 123 adult residents of a rural Canadian town, using a modified Affect Balance Scale to tap "more enduring affective states."   He defines happiness in terms of positive effect, negative effect, and long-term satisfaction.   No norms are presented.

Moriwaki (1974) administered the ABS to two samples of people 60 years and older: one (n=8) drawn from Los Angeles County mental health clinics and the second (n=19) consisting of church members who were judged by an informant to be mentally healthy. The mean for the normal sample was 8.27 (with the ABS scored 0-10) and the mean for the psychiatric sample was 4.25.

In a longitudinal study of the relationship between the happiness and social participation of older people, Graney (1975) administered the ABS to 46 elderly women aged 66-92. The distribution of the scores for the 44 who gave usable responses included 11 women who expressed a clear majority of positive feeling, 13 who exhibited a majority of negative feelings and 20 who fell into a middle category. Increments in activity were associated with happiness and decrements with unhappiness.

Measurement Properties

Reliability. Bradburn (1969) reports a test-retest correlation of .76 when a subsample of respondents were tested three days apart.

Validity. Bild and Havighurst (1976), in a study of elderly Chicagoans, show that the ABS correlates with an 18-item version of the LSI-A (r=.66). Moriwaki (1974) demonstrates that the ABS is significantly related to the Rosow Morale Scale (r=.61) and negatively related to a nine-item mental illness scale (r=.64). The ABS as a whole performed better than the subscales taken separately. In addition, Moriwaki demonstrates that the ABS significantly discriminated between normal and mentally troubled older persons.

Sensitivity to Change. Bradburn (1969) reports that the proportion of scores which change
across time "is substantially larger than we
would expect simply based on our reliability
estimates" (p. 83). This indicates that the
instrument is quite sensitive to change. Theoretically, affect is expected to be changeable;
thus, we would expect such sensitivity.

Appropriateness for Older Samples. Moriwaki
(1974) reports that ABS is "comprised of short
self-report items which can be easily administered to older subjects" (p. 73). Her findings,
as well as those of other investigators, suggest
that the ABS is applicable to older subjects.

Comments and Recommendations

There are distinct theoretical advantages to
use of the ABS. The scale permits the assessment
of positive affect, negative affect, and the
balance of the two. In addition, it permits the
quantification of amount of affect experienced
within the given time referent. Thus, subjects
may differ not only in the kind of feelings they
report, but also the frequency with which they
experience affect. The ABS is, in our opinion,
the best available measure of affect.

Essential Reference

Bradburn, N.M. The Structure of Psychological
   Well-Being. Chicago: Aldine Publishing
   Company, 1969.

This volume contains all essential information
on the development and standardization of the
ABS and presents the instrument in standard form.

Chapter 4

SELF-ESTEEM AND RELATED CONCEPTS

CONCEPTUAL AND METHODOLOGICAL ISSUES

The pursuit of self-knowledge is an important
tradition in Western civilization. The dictum
to "Know thyself" illustrates the value placed
upon personal insight as a component of meaningful life experience. For many of us, it is
difficult to believe that all could be right
with the world, unless all is simultaneously
right within ourselves. Katherine Mansfield
described the importance of self-understanding
in the last entry in her journal, written short-
ly before her death at the age of 34:

> I want, by understanding myself, to
> understand others. I want to be all
> that I am capable of becoming. . .
> This all sounds very strenuous and
> serious. But now that I have wrestled
> with it, it's no longer so. I feel
> happy--deep down. All is well.
> (Murray, 1927, p. 250)

Several bodies of theory and research inform social science perspectives on self-esteem. In the field of psychology, self-esteem has been an important component of the psychoanalytic theories of Fromm, Horney, Adler, and others; of the ego psychology of Allport; and of the clinical theories of Rogers and Maslow. In general, psychologists view self-esteem as an important component of individual personality, emphasizing the relationship between self-esteem and mental health or intrapsychic well-being. In the field of sociology, the role theory perspective of Secord and Backman, and the symbolic interactionist perspectives of Cooley, Mead, and Kuhn have devoted considerable attention to self-esteem. These sociological perspectives emphasize the critical role of social interaction and significant others in the development and maintenance of self-esteem. A detailed examination of these psychological and sociological perspectives is not possible here, but several recent, comprehensive reviews are available (Wells and Marwell, 1976; Wylie, 1974).

In conventional usage, self-esteem is defined as "self-respect or self-conceit", (Webster, 1968). Although "self-respect" comes closer to the definition of self-esteem we have in mind, neither of Webster's alternatives captures the essense of the term as it is used in social-psychological research. As it has been conceptualized in social-psychology, self-esteem refers to a basic feeling of self-worth--a belief that one is basically a person of value, acknowledging personal strengths and accepting personal weaknesses (Wells and Marwell, 1976; Rosenberg, 1965; Coopersmith, 1967). Positive or high self-esteem is viewed as a healthy component of personality, associated with interpersonal success and mastery. This is the definition that will be used in this chapter; a realistic and positive sense of self-worth is viewed as a subjective dimension of quality of life.

Social-psychological literature contains a variety of self-related terms including self-concept, self-image, self-acceptance, self-regard, and self-actualization. All of the terms are conceptually related to self-esteem in that they focus upon the personal perceptions individuals hold about themselves. The distinction between self-esteem and self-concept is crucial and will be discussed in the following paragraphs. Explicit definitions of the other self-related terms will not be presented here. The interested reader is referred to one of the excellent resources available in this substantive area (Wells and Marwell, 1976; Wylie, 1974).

The distinction made in this chapter between self-concept and self-esteem rests upon a view of the self which contrasts <u>cognitive</u> and <u>affective</u> or <u>evaluative</u> processes in self-perception. Self-concept is the cognitive component of the self and consists of the individual's perceptions of himself or herself as an object (i.e., what I am really like). Self-esteem consists of the affective judgments emerging from individuals' comparisons of what they are like to what they aspire to be like. According to this definition, self-concept is basically a descriptive phenomenon. Epstein, for example, refers to self-concept as the

theory an individual holds about himself or
herself as an object (1973). Self-esteem, on
the other hand, is evaluative and can be
assessed quantitatively (i.e., as "high" or
"low" as "positive" or "negative"). In the
past, numerous investigators have rated self-
concepts as "high" or "low", "positive" or
"negative". The distinction made in this
chapter restricts such evaluative ratings to
measures of self-esteem. For example, if a
person describes himself as being of average
intelligence, he has revealed nothing about
his self-esteem unless he mentions his ascribed
level of intelligence. This distinction between
self-concept as the cognitive component and
self-esteem as the affective or evaluative
component of the self is compatible with the
conceptual positions taken in several reviews
in this substantive area (Wells and Marwell,
1976; Crandall, 1973; Shaver, 1969; Gordon,
1968). In this chapter, we review measures of
self-esteem, which emphasize the affective
aspects of self-perception. It is important
to remember, however, that such self-evaluations
must be preceded by cognitive self-concept
processes (Lyons, 1977).

Both the definitions of self-esteem and
self-concept and the measuring instruments
presented in this chapter assume that self-
preceptions and self-evaluations are consciously
available to and can be accurately reported by
the individual. Wylie (1974) refers to this
as the "phenomenal view" of the self. This is
the predominant theoretical perspective currently taken in regard to these concepts. A
minority of theorists, however, view the self
as unconscious and, consequently, unable to be

measured using self-report instruments. As
Wylie points out, advocates of this viewpoint
find themselves unable to measure self-related
constructs at all. If self-esteem or self-
concept is not consciously available and yet
is an intrapsychic phenomenon, all possibilities
for measurement have been logically precluded.
It is our opinion that the viewpoint taken by
the majority of theorists and the volumes of
research findings based on this viewpoint
justify the measurement of self-esteem by self-
report methods. Certainly, most of us
intuitively assume a human capacity for self-
examination and evaluation.

The varied measures of self-esteem and
related constructs reflect, in part, the variety
of theoretical perspectives which incorporate
self-related concepts. While we have attempted
to consolidate pertinent issues, such efforts
are limited by the diversity of perspectives
which include self-esteem as a valuable concept.
Specific measurement instruments have been
developed to measure self-esteem in ways
compatible with the theoretical allegiancies
of their originators. Prospective research
investigators should carefully review the
theoretical assumptions which underlie the
construction of measures, assuring themselves
that these assumptions are compatible with
their own research questions. As is true with
any measure, measures of self-esteem should not
be blindly administered, but instead should be
chosen after prudent consideration of the theoretical issues and research question involved.

Thus far, self-esteem has been addressed as a global concept. That is, self-esteem refers to an individual's overall general sense of self-worth. Most measures of self-esteem adopt this generalized, global referent. One can also imagine, however, dimensions of self-esteem or domain-specific self-evaluations. For example, an individual could evaluate herself positively as a worker while judging herself quite negatively as a mother. The prospective researcher should carefully decide whether a global or a dimensional measure of self-esteem is best suited to the research question at hand. There are only a few existent dimensional measures of self-esteem; two of the best known have been included in our review. It should be noted, however, that several global measures of self-esteem have been demonstrated to be highly sensitive and predict behavior in previous research.

The stability of individual assessments of self-esteem remains an important unresolved theoretical and empirical issue. Some theorists, particularly psychologists, view self-esteem as a relatively enduring trait of the individual, largely impervious to factors in the social and personal environment. Other theorists, especially sociologists, view self-esteem as a more transitory social-psychological state, heavily dependent upon personal and situational factors. The question is perhaps best answered empirically. Unfortunately, an answer depends upon carefully constructed and analyzed longitudinal studies which, thus far, are lacking. Currently, it appears that some measures of self-esteem are more sensitive to change than others.

The "state-trait" debate has important implications for the use of self-esteem measures as outcome variables in evaluation research. To the degree that self-esteem is an enduring trait of the individual, it should be impervious to intervention, and hence an unsuitable criterion for program evaluation. If, on the other hand, self-esteem is responsive to changes in the external environment, two tasks remain before the effects of interventions on self-esteem can be clearly delineated. First, normative values for self-esteem across the life span should be determined. Second, the conditions with which self-esteem varies should be discerned.

Related to the change versus stability issue, is the question of age changes in self-esteem. Theoretically, the question is complex. If self-esteem is a stable individual characteristic, age changes are unlikely. If, on the other hand, self-esteem is situationally responsive, age changes are possible to the degree that important situational variables change with age. Although different theoretical perspectives suggest different determinants of self-esteem, none of these perspectives posit that self-esteem is a developmental phenomenon (i.e., that it is intrinsically linked to age or underlying biological mechanisms). It is quite possible that the determinants of self-esteem often change with age, but it is unlikely that age per se operates casually upon self-esteem. Empirical evidence thus far is somewhat ambiguous. A majority of studies report no age differences in self-esteem between older and younger subjects. The few

studies that do find significant age differences
report that older subjects exhibit higher levels
of self-esteem (Grant, 1966; Postema, 1970).
Longitudinal studies to determine age changes
in self-esteem over time are unavailable thus
far.   The position taken in this chapter is
that there are no compelling reasons to expect
age differences or age changes in self-esteem,
provided extraneous variables are appropriately
controlled.

The issue of age changes is also relevant
to the use of self-esteem measures as criterion
variables in evaluation research.   If age changes
were expected, the impact of an intervention
could become confounded with underlying developmental changes over time.

Although empirical evidence is scant, our
best guess is that self-esteem is situationally
responsive, and is not a developmental phenomenon.   To the degree that these two conclusions
are accurate, a sensitive measure of self-esteem
should be an adequate criterion for use in
intervention studies.

Instruments to be Reviewed

In this chapter, we review five selected
measures of self-esteem.   The Self-Esteem
Scale (Rosenberg, 1965) is included because
it is a unidimensional, extensively used, and
well documented measure of self-esteem that
has been administered to large and diverse
samples of children and adults of all ages.
The Self-Esteem Scale is perhaps the classic
measure of global self-esteem.   The Self-

Acceptance Scale (Berger, 1952) has been administered to samples of all ages, including older
subjects. Like the Self-Esteem Scale, it is an
easily administered, easily scored, global
measure of self-esteem. The Tennessee Self-
Concept Scale (TSCS) has several advantages,
including a global self-esteem scale, subscales
which describe more specific dimensions of self-
esteem and self-concept, and a measure of
self-criticism which serves as a useful check on
the potential confounding effects of defense
mechanisms and social desirability (Fitts, 1965).
The TSCS is in many ways a psychometric landmark
in the measurement of self-esteem and self-concept.
Although the Self-Esteem Inventory (Coopersmith,
1967) has had little use on older samples, we
include it as a potentially useful measure of
subjective life quality for older adults. Its
most attractive features include ease of administration and the fact that it taps four specific
domains of self-esteem. Finally, one semantic
differential measure is reviewed. This specific
measure (Monge, 1973) is included because it is
well documented in psychometric terms and has
been administered to subjects covering virtually
the whole life span. We review one semantic
differential measure because this is probably
the most frequently used approach to the measurement of self-esteem and self-concept in older
adults.

SELF-ESTEEM SCALE
(Rosenberg, 1965)

Description of Instrument

Rosenberg (1965) defines self-esteem as self-acceptance or a basic feeling of self-worth. The Self-Esteem Scale consists of ten items with responses reported along a four-point continuum from "strongly agree" to "strongly disagree". The measure was designed to be scored as a Guttman scale, and the four response categories are scored dichotomously as "agree" or "disagree". Some investigators, however, have used simple summing procedures rather than the Guttman scale format for scoring. (For a description of Guttman scaling techniques, see Nunnally, 1967). The instrument was intended to be brief (for ease of administration), global, and unidimensional.

Research Context and Use

Rosenberg (1965) developed the Self-Esteem Scale for a study of high school students. In that study, 5,024 high school students were randomly selected from ten public schools in New York City. Self-esteem scores were correlated with a variety of variables including family characteristics, interpersonal patterns, psychological states, occupational orientation, and participation and leadership in high school activities. In his 1965 volume, Rosenberg impressively describes the interpersonal contexts within which high and low levels of self-esteem are found among adolescents.

Robert Atchley (1969, 1976) and his colleagues
(Cottrell and Atchley, 1969) used the Self-
Esteem Scale in a study of adjustment to
retirement. The sample included 1,385 male and
2,167 female retirees selected from two broad
occupational categories--former public school
teachers and former telephone company employees.
The respondents typically reported very high
levels of self-esteem. The gender differences
were statistically significant, with men exhibiting higher self-esteem. Differences between
the two occupational groups were not significant.

Kaplan and Pokorny (1969) administered the
Self-Esteem Scale to 500 persons randomly
selected from the adult population of Harris
County, Texas (which includes Houston). Sixty-
five respondents were age 60 or older. The
authors report that age is unrelated to self-
esteem.

Ward (1977) administered the Self-Esteem
Scale to 323 community residents, age 60 to 92
in Madison, Wisconsin. The sample was slightly
above average in education, income, and health.
Ward reports that attitudes toward old age were
the best predictors of self-esteem for both men
and women in his sample. Additional significant
predictors of self-esteem for women were current
activities, age-related deprivations, and health.
For men, additional significant predictors of
self-esteem were income and education.

Measurement Properties

Reliability. Two kinds of reliability data
are available. In terms of internal consistency,

Rosenberg (1965) reports a Guttman scale reproducibility coefficient of .92 and a scalability coefficient of .72. Ward (1977) reports a coefficient of alpha of .74 and factor analysis conducted by Kaplan and Pokorny (1969) confirms that the Self-Esteem Scale is unidimensional. In terms of internal consistency, then, there is evidence of adequate reliability. In terms of test-retest reliability, Silber and Tippett (1965) report a correlation of .85 between measures administered to college students at two week intervals.

Validity. Evidence of convergent validity is provided by Silber and Tippett (1965), who report correlations ranging from .56 to .83 between the Self-Esteem Scale and other measures of self-esteem. Rosenberg (1965) reports considerable evidence of predictive validity, using a criterion group design. A group of 150 normal volunteers were administered the Self-Esteem Scale and were independently rated by a panel of nurses in terms of depression. Scores on the Self-Esteem Scale were significantly correlated with the nurses' ratings.

Sensitivity to Change. There is little evidence of the scale's sensitivity to change since, to our knowledge, it has not been longitudinally administered and analyzed.

Appropriateness for Older Samples. Available evidence suggests that the Self-Esteem Scale is appropriate for use with older respondents. The ease of administration and brevity of the instrument increase its attractiveness.

Comments and Recommendations

The Rosenberg Self-Esteem Scale appears to be
a valuable research tool for measuring global
self-esteem--for samples of all ages, including
older adults. Choice of an optimal scoring
format (e.g., Guttman scaling versus simple
summing) remains an unresolved issue in need of
further inquiry. Nonetheless, the instrument
is brief, easy to administer, and has well
documented measurement properties. As a measure
of global self-esteem, this instrument is
heartily recommended.

Essential Reference

Rosenberg, M. Society and the Adolescent Self-
    Image. Princeton, New Jersey: Princeton
    University Press, 1965.

This volume documents the development of the
Self-Esteem Scale and its earliest use.

SELF-ACCEPTANCE SCALE
(Berger, 1952)

Description of Instrument

According to Berger, the self-accepting person experiences feelings of self-worth, a belief in one's personal abilities, and adheres to internalized principles. In these terms, self-acceptance is similar to self-esteem as defined in this chapter and reflects the affective and evaluative components of self-perception.

The Self-Acceptance Scale consists of 36 items. Each item is answered along a five-point continuum of agreement ranging from "not at all true of myself" to "true of myself".

Research Context and Use

Berger (1952) designed the Self-Acceptance Scale to test the hypothesis that self-acceptance is positively related to acceptance of others. He administered the Self-Acceptance Scale to several groups of college students and adults. Mean levels of self-acceptance in these groups ranged from 102.00 to 142.63.   The potential range of scores is 36 to 180. As expected, Berger found support for his original hypothesis that acceptance of self correlates positively with acceptance of others.

Wolk (1976) and Wolk and Telleen (1976) administered the Self-Acceptance Scale to older subjects in two residential environments: a highly structured retirement home and a less structured retirement home. In these studies, self-acceptance as well as health, activity levels, developmental task accomplishment, and perceived autonomy were examined as predictors of life satisfaction and locus of control. As expected, residents of the less structured environment reported higher levels of life satisfaction and self-acceptance.

Measurement Properties

Reliability. Berger (1952) reports Spearman-Brown reliability coefficients--a measure of internal consistency--of .75 and greater. It should be noted that these coefficients were based on younger samples.

Validity. In terms of convergent validity, Omwake (1954) reports correlations of .49 between the Berger Self-Acceptance Scale and the Bills Self-Acceptance Index and .73 between the Berger Self-Acceptance Scale and Phillips Self-Acceptance Scale. Berger (1952) had 20 respondents write essays about themselves and take the Self-Acceptance Scale. As expected, scores on the Self-Acceptance Scale were highly correlated (r=.89) with judges' independent ratings of the essays. These validity data, however, also are based on younger samples.

Sensitivity to Change. There is no evidence for this as, to our knowledge, this scale has not been longitudinally administered.

Appropriateness for Older Samples. Based on the work of Wolk (1976) and Wolk and Telleen (1976), the Self-Acceptance Scale appears appropriate for administration to older persons.

It is also an easily administered instrument
with a straight forward response format, which
should increase its utility for older samples.

Comments and Recommendations

This instrument clearly requires more attention
in terms of its applicability for older people.
Normative data based on older samples should be
a priority issue.   Reliability and validity
information based on older samples also are
needed.   Suggestions for future use thus
include administration to larger, more heterogeneous samples of older persons and subsequent
item analysis for further refinement.   In
addition, longitudinal application of this
measure would yield useful information concerning the instrument's sensitivity to change.

In spite of these research needs, this
instrument appears to warrant further use with
older samples.   The ease of administration and
scoring is clearly one advantage of this measure.

Essential References

Berger, E.   The Relations Between Expressed
      Acceptance of Self and Expressed Acceptance
      of Others.   Journal of Abnormal and Social
      Psychology, 1952, 47, 778-782.

Berger, E.   Relations Among Acceptance of Self,
      Acceptance of Others, and MMPI Scores.
      Journal of Counseling Psychology, 1955,
      2, 279-284.

These references document the development of
the Self-Acceptance Scale and its earliest
applications.

TENNESSEE SELF-CONCEPT SCALE
(Fitts, 1965)

Description of Instrument

This instrument was developed specifically for clinical use. Fitts is interested in the potential of using self-esteem and self-concept—which he views as the individual's personal frame of reference—in mental health rehabilitation.

The Tennessee Self-Concept Scale (TSCS) consists of 100 items. Ninety self-descriptive statements were constructed by Fitts to fill fifteen cells in two dimensions, as indicated below:

	Self-Identity	Self-Acceptance	Behavior
Physical Self			
Moral-Ethical Self			
Personal Self			
Family Self			
Social Self			

The rows represent components of the external frame of reference, while the columns represent components of the internal frame of reference. Six items represent each cell, yielding 90 statements which are balanced for positivity and negativity. The response categories lie along a five-point continuum, ranging from

"completely false" to "completely true". The
total score for these 90 items is a Positive
Self-Esteem Score. Various subsets of these
items yield other measures such as a Self-
Actualization Score and a Personality Integration
Score. The interested reader is referred to
the manual for this instrument (Fitts, 1965)
for a complete catalog and description of these
subscales.

The ten remaining items are the Self-Criticism
Scale (L Scale) from the MMPI. These items are
mildly negative and most people score appropriately high on this scale. A suspiciously
low score on the Self-Criticism Scale should
caution the investigator that the 90 remaining
items may reflect defensive responses or the
effects of attempting to answer the questions
in socially desirable ways.

Research Context and Use

Fitts' theoretical approach to self-esteem
builds upon humanistic clinical psychology in
the tradition of Rogers and Maslow. Fitts
designed the TSCS as a tool for clinical research and rehabilitation. Fitts and his
colleagues have administered the scale to a
wide variety of samples, including juvenile
delinquents and respondents with diagnosed
psychopathology, as well as to normal subjects.

One of the difficulties in using this scale
is the fact that it is a commercial instrument,
consequently the instrument and scoring information must be purchased by users. In addition,
Fitts has published very little information
about the instrument, choosing instead to sell

a series of monographs through the commercial firm that markets his instrument. We will restrict discussion to the sample upon which the scale was developed and validated. Other samples are reported in Fitts 1971, 1972a, 1972b, 1972c, and Fitts and Hammer, 1969.

Fitts' (1965) initial sample consisted of 626 persons, aged 12-68. The sample included men and women, blacks and whites. The Positive Self-Esteem Score has a potential range of 90 to 450 and the mean in this sample was 345.57.

The TSCS has been used widely on diverse samples for a variety of research and clinical studies. We will focus upon studies of older persons which utilize the TSCS.

Grant (1966) explored age differences in a sample of 500 men and women, aged 20-69. She reports higher levels of positive self-esteem in older subjects, but also notes higher levels of denial among older respondents. She suggests that either denial is an important adaptive component of self-esteem in late life or that denial confounds the measurement of self-esteem among older persons.

Postema (1970) examined the relationships among time orientation, reminiscing, and self-esteem in a sample of older males. Specific comparisons were drawn between nursing home patients and community residents.

Crandall (1975) examined the relationships between health, age, income, and marital status and self-concept in a sample of middle class white men, aged 55 to 86.

Trimakas and Nicolay (1974) studied altruistic behavior as a function of self-esteem and social influence in a sample of 162 women, aged 66 to 88.   In the sample, the mean on Positive Self-Esteem was 380.89, significantly higher than the mean of Fitts' 1965 sample.   The mean on the Self-Criticism Scale was also significantly lower than that for Fitts' 1965 sample.   This supports Grant's 1966 finding that both denial and self-esteem are somewhat higher among older persons than among adults in general.

Measurement Properties

Reliability.   Fitts (1965) reports test-retest coefficients of .92 for the Positive Self-Esteem Score and .75 for the Self-Criticism Scale over a two week interval, in a study of 60 college students.

Validity.   In terms of convergent validity, Fitts   (1965) reports that the Positive Self-Esteem Scale correlates -.70 with the Taylor Manifest Anxiety Scale.   Thompson (1972) reports similar highly negative correlations with other measures of anxiety.   Fitts also reports that the Positive Self-Esteem Score correlates -.21 with the F Scale (a measure of authoritarianism), suggesting discriminant validity of the TSCS. In terms of predictive validity, Fitts and his colleagues have demonstrated the utility of the TSCS for distinguishing between mental health and psychopathology in a diverse range of samples.

Sensitivity to Change.   There is little evidence of the scale's sensitivity to change since, to our knowledge, it has not been long-itudinally administered and analyzed.

Appropriateness ·for Older Samples. Available
evidence suggests that this instrument is usable on samples of older adults. The reported
relatively high levels of denial (low Self-
Criticism scores) exhibited by older subjects
(Grant, 1966; Trimakas and Nicolay, 1974) should
caution the prospective user, however. Although
Trimakas and Nicolay (1974) suggest a positive
role for denial in the self-esteem of older
people, research investigators should use caution
in interpreting Positive Self-Esteem Scores for
respondents who score low on the Self-Criticism
Scale.

Comments and Recommendations

There are several very appealing aspects about
the TSCS. First, it is a scale which measures
both general self-esteem and more specific
aspects of the self. Second, the scale has been
extensively used with a diversity of samples.
The inclusion of the Self-Criticism Scale as a
check for defense or socially desirable responses
is a third advantage.

There are also areas, however, where further
refinement would be profitable. First, there
is need for more normative data on older samples.
Second, the existing evidence of increased denial
in older subjects requires careful scrutiny.
Finally, this scale would profit from systematic
longitudinal analysis to trace change over time
in both overall self-esteem and the various subscales. Nonetheless, this instrument is very
attractive and is highly recommended for
further use.

Essential Reference

Fitts, W. Tennessee Self-Concept Scale Manual.
  Nashville: Counselor Recordings and Tests,
  1965.

  This manual describes the development and
validation of the Tennessee Self-Concept Scale.

SELF-ESTEEM INVENTORY
(Coopersmith, 1967)

Description of Instrument

Coopersmith (1967) defines self-esteem as
self-judgments of personal worth. This conceptualization is compatible with the definition
of self-esteem presented in this volume.

The original version of the Self-Esteem Inventory included 50 items, but Coopersmith reduced
the scale to 25 statements on the basis of item
analysis. The 25-item instrument is discussed
here. The items are short statements which the
subject rates as either "like me" or unlike me".

Crandall (1973) reports that the scale is
multidimensional, including four factors:
leadership-popularity, self-derogation, family-
parents, and assertiveness-anxiety.

Research Context and Use

Coopersmith wished to identify the antecedents
and consequences of self-esteem in pre-adolescent
children. He hypothesized several kinds of antecedents including the individual's history of
success and failure; personal values, aspirations, and characteristic styles of coping with
criticism; and especially, interaction with
significant others. Coopersmith originally
administered the 50-item Self-Esteem Inventory
to 87 fifth-and sixth-grade children. The same
scale was subsequently administered to a more
heterogeneous sample of 1,748 children. Analysis
of data from the later study resulted in the 25-
item revision of the scale.

Coopersmith reports normative data for the two original samples (1967). Since the data are based on the 50-item measure and the respondents were all children, those data are not reproduced here. In general, both samples exhibited distributions of scores skewed in the direction of positive self-esteem. There were no significant differences in mean scores between male and female respondents.

The Self-Esteem Inventory has been widely used with many kinds of samples (Crandall, 1973, reviews these). To our knowledge, it has been used in only one study of older persons. Ernst and Kantor (1976) administered a 35-item version of the instrument in a study of the effects of a cosmetic program upon the self-esteem of institutionalized older women. Their sample consisted of 95 female residents of a nursing home. Neither a more detailed description of the sample nor normative data were reported.

Measurement Properties

Reliability. Coopersmith (1967) reports test-retest reliability coefficients of .88 over five weeks and .70 over three years, based upon his samples of pre-adolescent children. Taylor and Reitz (reported in Crandall, 1973) report a split-half reliability coefficient of .90. All these results are based on the 50-item original version of the scale, however. In general, the shorter length of the revised scale would be expected to reduce the reliability of the measure somewhat. In terms of internal consistency, Crandall (1973) reports inter-item correlations of the measure to be relatively low (average correlation of .13) in a sample of 453 college students. This suggests limited internal consistency; a consequence in part of the multidimensional nature of the measure.

Validity. In terms of convergent validity, Crandall (1973) reports correlations of .59 and .60 between the 25-item Self-Esteem Inventory and the Rosenberg Self-Esteem Scale in samples of college students. Ziller, Hagey, Smith, and Long (1969) correlated the Self-Esteem Inventory with the Bills Index of Adjustment and Values and the Ziller Social Self-Esteem Scale. For males, the correlations were .46 and .02 respectively.

In terms of discriminant validity, Taylor and Reitz (reported in Crandall, 1973) report correlations of .75 and .44 between the Self-Esteem Inventory and the Edwards and Marlowe-Crowne social desirability scales, respectively. The potential confounding of self-esteem and social desirability is a frequently voiced concern about measures of self-esteem.

Sensitivity to Change. Coopersmith (1967) reports a test-retest reliability of .70 after three years, suggesting relative stability over time. He claims that the Self-Esteem Inventory taps relatively stable, rather than more transitory, aspects of self-esteem.

Appropriateness for Older Samples. Although the measure has been administered to older respondents in only one known study, the form of the measure and the content of the items suggest that it could easily be administered to older subjects.

Comments and Recommendations

Clearly, the greatest disadvantages of this instrument in research with older subjects are the lack of normative data and validation upon older samples. Although this measure has been used in numerous studies, its suitability for older respondents remains largely unaddressed. In spite of this, the instrument appears potentially valuable and validation studies on older subjects are highly recommended. The multidimensional structure of the scale makes it a potentially attractive measure of domain-specific self-esteem.

Essential Reference

Coopersmith, S. The Antecedents of Self-Esteem. San Francisco: W.H. Freeman, 1967.

This volume describes the development and earliest applications of the Self-Esteem Inventory.

SEMANTIC DIFFERENTIAL SCALE
(Monge, 1973)

Overview of the Semantic Differential Technique

The semantic differential is a method of measuring the meaning of an object or event, including the self as an object. The technique has a rather complex conceptual foundation; consequently, before reviewing one particular semantic differential scale, we will describe the general technique.

The semantic differential technique was developed by Osgood and his colleagues (Osgood and Suci, 1955; Osgood, Suci, and Tannenbaum, 1957) and is a method of measuring the meaning of an object or event. Osgood and Suci used factor analysis to derive three general dimensions of meaning which they claim are common to all objects or events: evaluation, potency, and activity.

The semantic differential technique requires the individual to rate an object or event on a series of seven-point bipolar adjectives. The object or event is termed the referent (i.e., the phenomenon to be rated); the adjectives constitute the items. The format of response categories (one per adjective) is typically as follows:

Good ___ ___ ___ ___ ___ ___ ___ Bad
       1   2   3   4   5   6   7

By rating the object along the continuum, respondents report both the direction and the intensity of their feelings about the object.

Virtually hundreds of semantic differential measures have been used in social-psychological research. This proliferation of instruments results from the nearly infinite number of referents which can be assessed and the equally infinite sets of adjectives which potentially could be used to rate the referents.

Several approaches have been used to apply semantic differential measures to the measurement of self-esteem and self-concept. One approach is to score "potency" and "activity" items as indicators of self-concept and to use "evaluation" items as measures of self-esteem. Another frequently used alternative is to ignore the distinction between self-concept and self-esteem and sum item scores for a particular referent. The summed scores are then viewed as evidence of self-esteem or self-concept, depending upon the investigator's preference. The most common approach to the measurement of self-esteem is to present the same set of adjectives twice, requiring respondents to rate both their "actual self" and "ideal self". Scores on the items for the "actual self" are viewed as measures of self-concept. Discrepancy scores (i.e., ideal self score minus actual score) are viewed as measures of self-esteem. Although the use of discrepancy scores raises statistical problems (Cronbach and Furby, 1969), this practice is common.

Description of Instrument

This instrument is intended to measure "the connotative structure of the self concept" (Monge, 1975, p. 281). Self-concept is defined

as self-attitudes as elicited by rating a series
of 21 bipolar adjectives as they relate to the
referent, "My Characteristic Self".

Research Context and Use

Monge developed this semantic differential
scale to examine age and sex differences in
self-concept among adolescents (1973). In a
later work (1975), he examined age and sex
differences in the structure of self-concept
over the major portion of the life span. In
his 1975 study, Monge administered the Semantic
Differential Scale to 4,540 subjects aged 9-89,
of whom 335 were age 65 and older.

Monge's primary focus was the structure of
self-concept across age groups. His early
study (1973) indicated that, for adolescents,
the structure of self-concept could be described
by four dimensions empirically derived by
principal components factor analysis. In the
later study (1975), principal components factors
were extracted for each of the age-sex groups.
Substantial agreement in factor structure was
found across the ten groups; thus the scores
were combined and one grand factor analysis was
performed. Thus, he found no age differences in
the structure of self-concept. The four components extracted were: achievement/leadership,
congeniality/sociability, adjustment, and
masculinity/femininity.

Nehrke (1974) used the Semantic Differential
Scale to examine differences in actual and per-
cieved self-concept across three generations.
The instrument was administered to 25 female

generational triads. Subjects rated three
referents: self (actual self-concept) and the
other two generational units (perceived self-
concept). The average age of the daughters, all
college students, was 19 years; of the mothers,
47 years; and of the grandmothers, 74 years.
There were no significant differences in self-
concept across the three generations.

Nehrke et al. (1975) used an expanded version
of Monge's instrument to examine age differences
in self-concept and the relationships among
self-concept, life satisfaction, and locus of
control. The sample consisted of 99 men resid-
ing in a V.A. domiciliary setting and capable
of self-care. The semantic differential was
scored such that higher scores indicate more
positive self-evaluations. The investigators
report significant correlations between scores
on the Semantic Differential Scale and the following variables: age (r=.23), life satisfaction
(r=.48), and locus of control (r=.17).

Measurement Properties

Reliability and Validity. No evidence has
been reported about the reliability or validity
of the Semantic Differential Scale.

Sensitivity to Change. There is no evidence
of the scale's sensitivity to change since, to
our knowledge, it has not been longitudinally
administered and analyzed.

Appropriateness for Older Samples. Based upon
available evidence, the Semantic Differential
Scale appears usable on older samples.

Comments and Recommendations

This version of the semantic differential is potentially very useful. The substantial amount of factor analysis conducted by Monge provides useful information about the lack of age differences in the structure of self-concept. The use of the instrument upon a large sample covering virtually the entire potential age range is refreshing indeed. Nehrke et al. observed significant age differences in semantic differential scores in a sample of institutionalized men, although these differences may be confounded by differences in length of residence or other factors. The identification of domain-specific dimensions of self-esteem also is an important feature of this measure.

More work is clearly needed in the areas of reliability and validity to improve confidence in the instrument. Available evidence, however, suggests that this is a useful measure.

Essential References

Osgood, C.E. and Suci, G.J. Factor Analysis of Meaning. Journal of Experimental Psychology, 1955, 50, 325-328.

Osgood, C.E., Suci, G.J., and Tannenbaum, P. The Measurement of Meaning. Urbana, Illinois: University of Illinois Press, 1957.

These sources provide descriptions of the semantic differential technique in general.

Monge, R.H.   Developmental Trends in Factors of Adolescent Self-Concept. Developmental Psychology, 1973, 8, 382-393.

Monge, R.H. Structure of the Self-Concept from Adolescence Through Old Age. Experimental Aging Research, 1975, 1, 281-291.

These articles describe the development and earliest applications of Monge's Semantic Differential Scale.

Chapter 5

GENERAL HEALTH AND FUNCTIONAL STATUS

CONCEPTUAL ISSUES

Physical well-being is probably a necessary part of the foundation upon which more subjective dimensions of life quality rest. Physical well-being is even more important for older persons than for the rest of the population precisely because it is much more likely to be problematic. Compared to younger persons, older Americans tend to be chronically ill more often (U.S. Public Health Service, 1972), to spend proportionally more of their incomes on health care (Rice, Anderson, and Cooper, 1968), and to more frequently mention health and disability as major personal problems or fears (Louis Harris and Associates, 1975). Given this set of conditions, it is not surprising that health is an important variable in much gerontological research and that many service programs for older persons include some form of health care.

103

In spite of the importance of health to quality of life, there is no simple or straightforward way to define or measure health. Health is a multidimensional concept, with different dimensions suitable to different research questions and purposes. In a now classic paper on the problems of developing adequate measures of health, Sullivan (1966) persuasively makes this point,

> Health is often spoken of as if it were a directly observable characteristic existing within the individual, but measurement of health, in fact, requires selection from many potentially measurable characteristics of a person or a population. How the measure is to be used is one consideration in the selection of these indicators. Another, equally important, is the complex of circumstances surrounding the measurement process . . . There is little empirical justification for the assumption that a unidimensional continuum underlies and relates the measures referred to as healthy and unhealthy in different contexts. Health, defined without reference to a specific situation or purpose of measurement, may be merely a verbal artifact. (p. 5-6)

In this chapter, we will examine several kinds of health and functional status measures. Health is typically defined as positive well-being--physical and emotional--and thus is more than the absence of disease. Functional status refers to the individual's ability to function independently and focuses upon self-care activities and mobility

limitations. Special emphasis will be given to
the relative advantages and disadvantages of
various measurement approaches and to the research
purposes for which they appear most appropriate.
As a concept to be defined and measured, health
highlights the recurring theme of the importance
of a well-articulated theoretical framework for
research. It is only with adequate theoretical
guidance that an appropriate measurement instrument can be chosen.

APPROACHES TO THE MEASUREMENT OF
PHYSICAL HEALTH AND FUNCTIONAL STATUS

Four major approaches have been used to define
and measure physical health or functional status
in social research, not including the ratings
of physicians. Each of these approaches has also
been used in the study of late life. At least
one instrument from each approach will subsequently be reviewed; at this point the approaches
will be briefly described and evaluated.

Subjective Health Ratings

Although physical health is certainly an objective phenomenon, most of us have a subjective
assessment of our own health status. If asked,
we are able to relate our health concerns and
to evaluate our physical well-being. Thus, health
is a subjective as well as an objective dimension
of life quality.

In social gerontology, subjective health
ratings are used more frequently than objective
measurement approaches. Several reasons for this
include the ease of administering self-rated

health measures, the low cost of such measures, and the demonstrated significant relationship between subjective health ratings and the ratings of physicians (cf. Maddox and Douglass, 1973). These, then, are the advantages of the subjective measurement approach.

Subjective health ratings have several limitations, however. First, and most important, it is not clear exactly what subjective health ratings measure. Although related to objective (i.e., physician's) health ratings, subjective health ratings are not synonomous with such measures. Because it is theoretically unclear what it is that such ratings measure, validation is virtually doomed. In addition, such measures may be unreliable and relatively insensitive to change. The status of subjective health ratings is thus theoretically, psychometrically, and empirically ambiguous.

The appropriate usage of subjective health ratings is an unanswered question. Although such ratings have been demonstrated to be modestly predictive of various attitudinal states and behaviors in late life, the causal order of such relationships remains problematic. Perhaps subjective health ratings are best used as a control variable in studies where the investigator wishes to eliminate the confounding effects of health. In such studies, the investigator may wish to use an inexpensive, convenient measure of health and may be prepared to tolerate a less objective and well-understood measure of health. Subjective health ratings are not useful for measuring the distribution or incidence of illness or degree of illness limitation or disability.

The status of subjective health measures has
been well summarized by Maddox and Douglass
(1973):

> Self-rating of health cannot serve as a
> substitute for epidemiologic diagnoses.
> These ratings clearly measure something
> more--and something less--than objective
> ratings. However, our data demonstrate
> that self assessment of health is not
> random but is persistently and positively
> related to objective evaluations of health
> status. Self ratings of health clearly
> have some utility as a measure of health
> in research involving older persons
> when objective measurements of health
> are not feasible. Furthermore, these
> data confirm that, in regard to evalua-
> tion of health, older people have and
> maintain a strong reality orientation.
> (p. 92)

Symptom or Illness Inventories

This measurement approach relies upon respondents' self-reports of symptoms or illnesses.
Typically such measures include a list of ailments
and subjects are asked to report whether or not
they suffer from them. Illness inventories are
relatively inexpensive and convenient to administer. In addition, they are more objective
than subjective health ratings and are theoretically less ambiguous.

In spite of these advantages, the use of such
measures is often problematic. The reliable
reporting of specific illnesses depends to some
degree upon the diagnostic experience of the

respondent. In order to accurately report an
illness, the respondent should ideally have
(a) been examined by an appropriate health care
professional, (b) have been told the diagnosis
in detail, and (c) have understood and remem-
bered the diagnosis. Unfortunately, it is
impossible to insure that each respondent has
completed each of these steps.

Secondly, there is the question of what
one really knows after being told that a
person suffers from a particular illness.
The prognostic severity of a given illness
often does not correlate highly with the
behavioral impact of the condition (i.e.,
some non-serious illnesses are painful and
disabling while some life-threatening conditions have little impact on ability to
function). There have been recent efforts
to calcuate physical health by weighting
various illnesses in terms of prognostic
outlook and effect upon functional performance (cf., Patrick, Bush, and Chen,
1973), but such efforts are still in the
exploratory stage and appear expensive,
time consuming, and complex.

The appropriate uses of illness inventories remain unclear. Most illnesses suf-
fered by older persons are chronic conditions which are unlikely to be "cured" in
an absolute sense. Thus, a check list of
illnesses is unlikely to be a useful criterion in an intervention study, as change
in presence or absence of the disease
typically cannot be expected. Certainly
such measures are not suitable for epidemiological or health planning purposes.

Perhaps the most appropriate use of such measures is to classify individuals into broad categories of health status, using more objective self-reports than those available with subjective health ratings.

Measures of Physical Functional Status

Functional status is one component of the larger, more amorphous concept, health. Functional status includes such factors as mobility; the ability to perform expected role duties, self-maintenance, and preferred activities; and general energy level. Measures of functional status thus emphasize the effects of disease rather than the existence of disease.

Most measures of physical functional status are self-report measures; subjects are asked to report activity limitations, difficulties in mobility and self-care, and ability to perform expected social roles. These instruments typically yield total scores representing degree of functional disability, and in some cases, subscores which are dimension specific.

There are several advantages to the use of functional status measures. First, the theoretical framework is well articulated--such measures reflect the physical ability of the individual to perform expected roles and activities. For many social research questions, especially research questions about the physical well-being of older people, these behavioral aspects of functional status are precisely the health dimension of interest. Secondly, measures of functional status are probably that component of health most sensitive to change and hence best suited for use as a criterion in intervention studies (Reynolds, Rushing, and Miles, 1974; Sullivan, 1966). Finally, although measures of physical functional status are somewhat longer than subjective health ratings or illness inventories, they can be obtained through self-reports; thus they are relatively inexpensive and easy to administer.

There is one potential problem in the use of functional status measures with older respondents. As Lawton, Ward, and Yaffe (1967) point out,

> Old age presents unique problems in measuring health, even when one limits oneself to a definition in terms of disability. Relatively objective indices of disability are available when one determines how much school a child misses, how many work days a man is disabled, or how many days a housewife can do no housework, but what is the appropriate role criterion for an older person? (p. 341)

While the question of expected role duties for older persons is theoretically problematic (Rosow, 1974), most measures of functional status emphasize the capacity for independent living (e.g., self-care, mobility)--a capacity that is certainly relevant to the life quality of older persons.

Multidimensional Measures of Functional Status

This measurement approach includes the assessment of physical functional status, but is more comprehensive, also including such factors as mental health status, quality of interpersonal

relationships, and social and economic resources.
The theoretical background for such measures
acknowledges the matrix of biological, psychological, and social factors that contribute
to general functional status.

The comprehensiveness of multidimensional
measures permits the investigator to monitor
complex patterns and interrelationships.
Such measures are thus potentially valuable
for creative research.   Several multidimensional measures have been well documented
in terms of reliability, validity, and
sensitivity to change.

The administration of multidimensional
measures of functional status is typically
expensive, time consuming, and frequently
requires the services of well-trained interviewers and raters.   Thus, multidimensional
measures of functional status should be
used with an eye to pragmatic concerns--
they may be worth the investment required
for their use only in special cases where
comprehensive, multidisciplinary data are essential to the research question.   Such measures
are potentially very useful in comprehensive
studies which focus upon functional status
and its correlates.

MENTAL HEALTH:
ANOTHER DIMENSION OF GENERAL HEALTH

The discussion thus far has focused largely
upon physical health.   Mental health, of course,
represents an additional important dimension
of general health which merits attention.

In this society, most mental health assessment is performed by mental health professionals in diagnostic interviews and, to a lesser degree, using standardized tests. Self-report measures of mental illness are relatively rare, although the major personality tests include dimensions which measure certain types of psychopathology. A detailed discussion of the measurement of mental health is outside the purview of this chapter. We will focus briefly on the possibilities of obtaining general information about mental health status from relatively short, self-report instruments.

Self-report measures of mental health have been developed primarily for epidemiological surveys of the prevalence of mental disorder in the community. A substantial amount of work has been done in this area (cf., Gurin, Veroff, and Feld, 1960; Hollingshead and Redlich, 1958), and at least one major study has been longitudinally applied (Srole, Langner, Michael, Opler, and Rennie, 1962; Srole, 1975). One frequently-used self-report measure of mental illness developed in this epidemiological tradition will be reviewed in this chapter.

Self-report measures of mental health face unusual problems of validation. The scope and symptoms of mental disorder are so broad that there is little liklihood that any instrument of reasonable length could be a valid and reliable indicator of mental illness. Available measures tend to be relatively crude and, appropriately, do not presume to be valid diagnostic tools for classification of type or degree of mental disorder. In spite of these limitations, several self-report measures of mental illness

have been demonstrated to be useful and valid,
at least in terms of general psychological dis-
tress.   The application of such instruments is
potentially useful, given that scores on such
measures are interpreted with caution.

Methodological Issues

Two methdological issues are particularly
pertinent to the measurement of general health
and functional status among older people. First,
various measures of health and functional status
tend to be developed, administered, and validated
on one of two types of samples--community residents living independently or institutionalized
individuals.   Rarely are the measures tested on
both community and institutionalized samples.
This becomes important to the potential research
investigator in two ways.   First, it cannot be
assumed that a measure which has been validated
for one kind of sample is equally appropriate
to the other kind of sample.   This is not to
say that future administration of the instrument
should be restricted to the original type of
sample.   Rather, investigators should exercise
caution in the interpretation of data and should
attempt to demonstrate the measure's suitability
to other kinds of samples.   Secondly, this issue
is particularly important in longitudinal or
intervention studies, where subjects are likely
to change status (e.g., move in and out of
hospitals or nursing homes).   In such cases,
it is essential that the health measure be
appropriate for use regardless of subject
status.

A second methodological issue concerns the
existence of "age-fair" tests of general health

and functional status, a specific aspect of the broader issue of appropriateness to older samples. Many measures of health have been developed to be optimally suitable to a particular age group (e.g., children, the older population). Because various age groups are likely to suffer particular kinds of illnesses or health conditions (e.g., acute illnesses are more common in the young, while chronic illnesses are more prevalent among older persons), a measure which is adequate for one age group may be inadequate for another age group. In general, illness inventories are less likely to be age-fair than are measures of functional status. This issue is relevant to broad scale surveys of health status, to studies of age differences in health status, and to longitudinal studies which cover a substantial portion of the life span.

INSTRUMENTS TO BE REVIEWED

In this chapter, five measures of physical health or functional status and one mental health measure will be reviewed. As least one measure is presented for each of the measurement approaches described above.

A general measure of subjective health is presented first. Such subjective health ratings have been frequently used in gerontological research. Second, the Health Index developed by Rosencranz and Pihlblad (1970) is described. This measure illustrates the use of an illness inventory with older subjects. Third, the Function Status Index is reviewed. Reynolds, Rushing, and Miles (1974) developed this instrument to measure physical functional status in individuals

of all ages. Two multidimensional measures of
functional status are reviewed. The first is
the OARS Multidimensional Functional Assessment
Questionnaire (OMFAQ). This instrument yields
a comprehensive evaluation of functional status
along several dimensions and has been validated
upon both community and institutionalized samples
(Duke Center for the Study of Aging, 1978). The
second multidimensional measure of functional
status is the Stockton Geriatric Rating Scale
(SGRS). This instrument is designed specifically
for institutionalized subjects and hence stresses
relatively extreme forms of impairment (Meer and
Baker, 1966). Unlike the other measures reviewed
in this volume, the SGRS is not a self-report
measure; instead it is an observational rating
scale. The SGRS and the related Geriatric Rating
Scale (Plutchik et al., 1970) are included
because of the special issues involved in testing
severely impaired, institutionalized subjects.
Finally, Langner's (1962) Twenty-Two Item Screening Scale is reviewed as a self-report measure
of mental health. This instrument is probably
the most frequently used measure of mental illness in survey research.

SUBJECTIVE HEALTH RATING

Description of Instrument

Subjective health is the individual's perception and evaluation of his or her overall health status. This instrument is a single item self-rating, with responses typically reported along a four or five point continuum from "poor" to "excellent." Thus, the measure yields ordinal data. This measure has a long and, in many ways, uncharted history in social science research. Consequently, it is impossible to attribute this instrument to any specific author.

Research Context and Use

The Subjective Health Rating has a long history in social science research. In social gerontology, Suchman, Phillips, and Streib (1958) report one of the first systematic examinations of subjective health assessment among older people. They administered the Subjective Health Rating to 3,623 men, age 65 and older, participating in a panel study of retirement. The study included global subjective health ratings, specific health attitudes, health-related behaviors, and physicians' ratings of these older men.

Shanas (1962) reports the distribution of Subjective Health Ratings in a sample of 1,734 men and women age 65 and older. This sample represented a random cross-section of the total non-institutionalized older population of the continental United States. In that study, 52.6

percent of the respondents rated their health as good; 28.3 percent as fair; and 19.2 percent as poor.

Tissue (1972) administered the Subjective Health Rating to 256 male and female welfare recipients with a median age of 68 years. In this sample, 33 percent reported enjoying good health, 46 percent reported fair health, and 21 percent felt they were in poor health.

The two Duke University longitudinal studies of aging permit the assessment of age changes in Subjective Health Ratings. Duke Longitudinal Study I was a twenty-two year panel study of older community residents. At the first round of data collection, the sample consisted of 256 black and white, male and female respondents, age 60 to 94. This distribution of Subjective Health Ratings for the 182 subjects present for the first two rounds of data collection are reported in Heyman and Jeffers (1963). Subjective Health Ratings also were collected in Duke Longitudinal Study II. This study includes four test dates at two year intervals. The original sample consisted of 502 white men and women, aged 46-71. A four-point response continuum, ranging from "poor" (1) to "excellent" (4) was used. Normative data for the 350 respondents tested at all four rounds are presented below:

	Mean	Standard Deviation
Round 1	2.90	.72
Round 2	3.05	.66
Round 3	3.04	.68
Round 4	2.99	.70

Measurement Properties

Reliability. Using data from Duke Longitudinal
Study I, Maddox and Douglass (1973) report test-
retest correlations ranging from .32 to .65 at
two-year intervals. In Duke Longitudinal Study
II, test-retest correlations at two-year intervals
range from .42 to .71. These correlations are
moderate, suggesting that either the item is not
very reliable or that significant changes have
occurred in these samples over the two-year interval. Unfortunately, particularly in the case
of single-item measures, true change cannot be
distinguished from unreliability.

Validity. Suchman et al. (1958), Maddox (1962),
and Friedsam and Martin (1963) report highly
significant relationships between Subjective
Health Ratings and physicians' ratings. Heyman
and Jeffers (1963) and Maddox and Douglass (1973)
further note that these relationships remain
stable over time.

Suchman et al. (1958) and Friedsam and Martin
(1963) report significant relationships between
Subjective Health Ratings and (a) health attitudes
(e.g., worry about health) and (b) health behavior
(e.g., activity limitations due to health problems). Similarly, Tissue (1972) reports a number
of significant associations between subjective
health and other health-related variables:

Correlate of Subjective Health	Gamma
Perception of recent health decline	.78
Own health compared to peers	.77
Worries about health	.73
Functional health index	.66

Correlate of Subjective Health, continued

Correlate of Subjective Health	Gamma
Number of health problems	.50
Last time saw a doctor	.36
Last time in a hospital	.31

The relationship between Subjective Health Ratings and morale has been of particular concern to social gerontologists. Some authors have hypothesized that Subjective Health Ratings are indicators of morale rather than a dimension of health. Suchman et al. (1958), Friedsam and Martin (1963), Maddox (1962), Maddox and Douglass (1973), and Tissue (1972) all report significant relationships between subjective health assessments and various measures of morale or related concepts. These correlations are typically moderate in magnitude, however (e.g., .50 or less in the Maddox and Douglass study and .45 or less in Tissue's study). Subjective Health Ratings thus are not merely measures of morale.

Sensitivity to Change. Evidence concerning the sensitivity of Subjective Health Ratings to change is ambiguous at best. The Duke Longitudinal studies indicate considerable stability of group means and distributions over time. The test-retest correlations in these same data are moderate, however. Given available data, two alternatives are equally possible. Either Subjective Health Ratings are relatively unreliable but stable over time, or they are highly sensitive to change but form similar distributions over time. If asked to make a guess, we would hypothesize the former--that Subjective Health

Ratings are unreliable rather than sensitive to change.

   Appropriateness for Older Samples. Subjective Health Ratings appear usable for older samples.

Comments and Recommendations

   Subjective Health Ratings are potentially compromised in several ways. Methodologically, the evidence is discouraging--the item is probably unreliable, its validity is dubious, and, if it is sensitive to change, that sensitivity cannot be separated from unreliability. In many ways this instrument embodies and illustrates the problems associated with the use of single-item measures.

   A Subjective Health Rating is not (a) a physician's health rating, (b) morale, (c) the number of health problems from which one suffers, or (d) one's attitudes toward or experience with the medical profession--although it is related to all these things. While we know what a Subjective Health Rating isn't, it is not all that clear what it is.

   In spite of this, Subjective Health Ratings appear to constitute one dimension of the broad concept called "health." Given the inability to objectively measure health status (i.e., obtain physicians' ratings) in many studies and the available evidence which suggests that Subjective Health Ratings are often predictive, we anticipate continued use of Subjective Health Ratings, but urge investigators to use restraint in the application and interpretation of this measure.

Essential Reference

Maddox, G.L. and Douglass, E.B.   Self-Assessment of Health: A Longitudinal Study of Elderly Subjects. Journal of Health and Social Behavior, 1973, 14, 87-93.

This reference provides a good overview of the uses and correlates of Subjective Health Ratings.

HEALTH INDEX

(Rosencranz and Pihlblad, 1970)

Description of Instrument

Physical health is conceptualized as the number and types of illnesses experienced within a specified time interval. In addition, length of illness and degree of confinement are included as important illness indicators. Thus, this measure taps self-reports of illness, rather than health per se.

The Health Index includes two components. First, respondents examine a list of 40 illnesses or medical conditions common among older people and report which ones they currently have. Second, subjects report specific health problems experienced in the past four weeks and the degree and length of confinement resulting from those recent health problems. Type of illness, length of confinement, and type of confinement are weighted in the calculation of index scores.

The authors caution potential users that the Health Index is designed solely for the purpose of classifying individuals into broad health classes. They specifically disclaim its appropriateness as a diagnostic tool or a device for health counseling.

Research Context and Use

The Health Index was designed as a self-report measure of physical health that would be more objective than Subjective Health Ratings

(Rosencranz and Pihlblad, 1970). The index was
first administered to a sample of 1,700 noninstitutionalized persons age 65 and older.
The sample comprised a stratified random cross-
section of Missouri residents.

Scores on the Health Index ranged from 0 (no
ailments) to 45.5. The scores were then divided
into five ordinal classes, where Class I indicated no illnesses and Class V represented persons reporting two or more serious conditions
and confinement to a hospital for part of the
previous month. Normative data, including the
sex and age distributions of the Health Index
are detailed in Rosencranz and Pihlblad (1970).

Measurement Properties

Reliability. No evidence is reported concerning the reliability of the Health Index.
There is general evidence, however, that recall
of illness tends to be unreliable (Mechanic,
1968). In addition, as Rosencranz and Pihlblad
note, self-reports of health conditions are
undoubtedly influenced by diagnostic exposure.
Thus, persons in frequent contact with health
care professionals can report their illnesses
more accurately than persons who infrequently
receive health services. In all likelihood,
the accuracy of illness reports also varies
by level of education.

Validity. There is limited evidence of the
validity of the Health Index. The Health Index
was significantly related to Subjective Health
Ratings and three indicators of functional
ability--specifically, ability to walk stairs,
to cut one's own toe nails, and to independently

wash and bathe (Rosencranz and Pihlblad, 1970).

Sensitivity to Change. There is no evidence
of the Health Index's sensitivity to change
since, to our knowledge, it has not been longitudinally administered.

Appropriateness for Older Samples. Based
upon the experience of Rosencranz and Pihlblad
(1970), the Health Index appears usable on
samples of older persons. The index was designed
for use on older samples and given the specific
health conditions included, it would not be
suitable for use with younger respondents.

Comments and Recommendations

There are several negative features to the
Health Index. It has had limited administration
and analysis, thus evidence concerning its
psychometric properties is scant. In particular,
more evidence is needed in the areas of reliability, validity, and sensitivity to change.
The instrument is not suitable for measuring
age differences in health, since it includes
those illnesses most common in old age and would
not be appropriate for younger subjects. The
Health Index probably would not be suitable for
use as a criterion variable for intervention
studies. Most of the health conditions in the
index are chronic conditions that are unlikely
to be cured. Finally, the health conditions
are dichotomized into major and minor illnesses.
This dichotomous treatment of illness severity
is fairly crude.

It is important to note that many of these
limitations are true of all illness inventories

and are not unique to the Health Index.   In
spite of the disadvantages, then, the Health
Index is probably the best available measure
which is based upon self-reports of illness.
We concur with Rosencranz and Pihlblad that the
Health Index is best suited for "establishing
relative categories of health status when
clinical examinations of many respondents is
neither practical nor possible" (1970, p. 133).

Essential Reference

Rosencranz, H.A. and Pihlblad, C.T.   Measuring
    the Health of the Elderly.   Journal of Geron-
    tology, 1970, 25, 129-133.

    This article describes the development and
early application of the Health Index.

FUNCTION STATUS INDEX

(Reynolds, Rushing, and Miles, 1974)

Description of Instrument

Functional status is defined as "the degree to which an individual is able to perform socially allocated roles free of medically-related limitations" (Reynolds et al., 1974). The authors clearly distinguish functional status from general health. Functional status is directly related to the ability to perform social roles, while a measure of general health need not take this into account.

The Function Status Index consists of four dimensions: movement, mobility, self-care activity, and role activity. Respondents indicate the degree of health-related dysfunction or impairment along specified continuua for each dimension. Scores can be summed across dimensions or calculated separately for particular dimensions of interest.

Research Context and Use

In a study designed to validate the Function Status Index, Reynolds et al. (1974) administered the index to random samples in two rural, economically depressed counties in Northern Alabama. The sample provided data for 8,036 individuals. Only one person per household was interviewed; however, the respondent provided data for other family or household members as well as himself or herself. The sample of interviewed respondents consisted of 2,629 persons. Distributions of

functional status or other normative data are
not reported.

Measurement Properties

Reliability. No data regarding the reliability of the Function Status Index have been
reported.

Validity. Reynolds et al. (1974) report
significant correlations between scores on the
Function Status Index and several health-related
variables. For the total sample of all individuals (n=8,036), the correlation between Subjective
Health Ratings and Function Status Index is .59;
for the sample of interviewed respondents (n=
2,629), the correlation is .72. The Function
Status Index also was significantly related to
the number of health care contacts in the previous two weeks (gamma values of -.53 and -.42
for the total sample and interviewed respondents,
respectively) and to worries about health problems (gamma values of -.48 and -.42).

Sensitivity to Change. There is no evidence
of the index's sensitivity to change since, to
our knowledge, it has not been longitudinally
administered and analyzed.

Appropriateness for Older Samples. Given the
experience of Reynolds et al., the Function
Status Index appears usable on older samples.
It should be noted that the Role Activity dimension of functional status is phrased and coded
in terms of age-related role activities (i.e.,
work and school). It is not clear, however,
what constitutes an appropriate range of activities for older people. Thus Reynolds et al.

report some difficulty evaluating functional status of older respondents on the dimension of role activity.

Comments and Recommendations

The Function Status index appears to be a useful measure of general physical status.   In general, measures of physical functional status are probably more sensitive to change than Subjective Health Ratings or illness inventories and hence better criterion measures for intervention studies.   On the other hand, as Reynolds et al. note, the Function Status Index would be inappropriate for some research purposes.   For example, scores on the Function Status Index would not help to identify the specific health care needs of individuals or groups since diverse medical conditions may be associated with a given level of disability.

The Function Status Index would profit from diverse administration.   In particular, further efforts are needed to evaluate reliability, validity, and sensitivity to change.   Nonetheless, the Function Status Index appears to be a potentially useful measure of physical functional status.

Essential Reference

Reynolds, W.J., Rushing, W.A. and Miles, P.L. The Validation of a Function Status Index. Journal of Health and Social Behavior, 1974, 15, 271-288.

This article describes the development and application of the Function Status Index.

OARS MULTIDIMENSIONAL
FUNCTIONAL ASSESSMENT QUESTIONNAIRE

(Duke University Center for the Study of
Aging and Human Development, 1978)

Description of Instrument

The OARS Multidimensional Functional Assessment Questionnaire is one component of a larger OARS instrument (Center for the Study of Aging and Human Development, 1978; Pfeiffer, 1975). The other component consists of a questionnaire measuring the use of sixteen types of generic services. Together, the OMFAQ and the services utilzation questionnaire comprise a model for assessing the impact of services, with functional status conceptualized as the criterion. The OMFAQ can be used independently as a measure of functional status.

The OMFAQ was designed to measure the current functional status of individuals or populations in five dimensions: social resources, economic resources, physical health, mental health, and capacity for self care and independent instrumental behavior or activities of daily living (ADL). Each dimension yields a functional status score which lies along a six-point continuum from "excellent" or "totally impaired." A cumulative rating of functional status also is calculated. The OMFAQ is suitable for either institutional or community residents.

The OMFAQ consists of 72 questions answered by the respondent; an additional ten questions about the respondent, answered by an informant;

fourteen questions about the respondent, answered by the interviewer; and five major rating
scales calculated by a rater. The portion of
the questionnaire answered by the respondent includes both objective and subjective questions.

Research Context and Use

The OMFAQ was developed in a series of
studies at the Duke Center for the Study of
Aging and Human Development and, from the
beginning, was intended as a measure useful
for purposes of clinical assessment, service
planning, and program evaluation. The first
problem addressed by OARS investigators was
that of alternatives to institutionalization,
including the effectiveness and cost of such
alternatives. The investigators soon broad-
ened their scope to include the related
issues of the epidemiology of functional
impairment in the older population and the
types and patterns of services available in
the community.

The OMFAQ was developed, validated, and
analyzed in an ongoing study of three older populations: (1) the Community Sample (n=997), a
random sample of ten percent of Durham County,
North Carolina residents age 65 and older, (2)
the Clinic Sample (n=98), a group of older persons
referred to the OARS clinical program for medical
or psychiatric treatment, and (3) the Institutional Sample (n=102), a twenty percent sample
of all institutionalized persons age 65 and older
in Durham County. The distributions of impairment in each of the five dimensions of functional status for these samples are presented
in Table 5.1.

TABLE 5.1

Percent of Impaired Respondents, by Dimension

Dimension	Durham Community Sample	Durham Clinic Sample	Durham Institutional Sample
Social Resources	9	41	66
Economic Resources	14	45	49
Mental Health	13	81	71
Physical Health	25	49	60
ADL	21	60	93

Source: E. Pfeiffer (Ed.) Multidimensional Functional Assessment: The OARS Methodology, A Manual. Durham, NC: Duke University Center for the Study of Aging and Human Development, 1975, pp.63-70.

131

Measurement Properties

Reliability. Fillenbaum (1978) has examined
both the test-retest and inter-rater reliability
of the OMFAQ. Table 5.2 presents the test-retest
correlations for the five dimensions of functional
status for the Durham Community Sample, based on
administrations of the questionnaire five weeks
apart. The test-retest correlations indicate
that objective items tend to be more reliable
than subjective items. All of the dimensions
except Mental Health appear adequately reliable
over the five week interval.

Since the OMFAQ depends heavily upon the
judgments of raters, both inter-rater reliability
(agreement among different raters) and intra-
rater reliability (agreement of the same rater
over time) have been examined (Fillenbaum, 1978).
Fillenbaum reports inter-rater reliabilities for
the Community Sample questionnaires ranging from
.38 to .88 for raters of mixed disciplinary
backgrounds and from .70 to .93 for raters of
the same disciplinary background. As expected,
inter-rater reliability was higher among raters
with the same professional background and among
more thoroughly trained raters. Also using the
Community Sample questionnaires, intra-rater
reliability coefficients ranged from .47 to 1.00
on ratings repreated after a 12 to 18 month interval. It appears that well-trained raters
can reliably evaluate the OMFAQ.

Validity. Two major kinds of validity data
for the OMFAQ have been reported by Fillenbaum
(1978). First, scores on the Physical Health
and Mental Health dimensions of the OMFAQ were
correlated with the independent assessments of

TABLE 5.2

Test-Retest Correlations for Five Dimensions
of Functional Status,
Durham Community Sample

Dimension	r
Social Resources	
Objective Items	.71**
Subjective Items	.53**
Economic Resources	
Subjective Items	.79**
Mental Health	
Life Satisfaction (Subjective Items)	.42*
Mental Health (Subjective Items)	.32
Physical Health	
Subjective Items	.59*
ADL	
Instrumental (Objective Items)	.72**
Physical (Objective Items)	.81**

*p ≤ .05
**p ≤ .001

SOURCE: G.G. Fillenbaum. Validity and Relia-
bility of the Multidimensional Functional
Assessment Questionnaire. In Duke University
Center for the Study of Aging and Human Develop-
ment, Multidimensional Functional Assessment:
The OARS Methodology, A Manual, (second edition).
Durham, NC: Duke University Center for the Study
of Aging and Human Development, 1978, p. 30.

physician's assistants and psychiatrists, respectively. The Spearman correlations between
OMFAQ scores and physician's assistants' ratings
on Physical Health ranged from .61 to .81. The
corresponding correlations between OMFAQ scores
and psychiatrists' ratings on Mental Health
ranged from .49 to 1.00.

Second, the OMFAQ has been shown to discriminate between known groups of community residents,
clinic patients, and institutional residents.
This pattern is shown in Table 5.1 presented
earlier, and is even more obvious in Table 5.3.

Sensitivity to Change. Although the OMFAQ
has been administered longitudinally to
Durham and Cleveland samples, explicit information concerning its sensitivity to change has
not been reported.

Appropriateness for Older Samples. The OMFAQ
was explicitly developed and refined on samples
of older persons and for purposes of planning
and evaluating services for the elderly.

Comments and Recommendations

The OMFAQ is an attractive measure of general
functional status. Among its advantages are the
following:

1. The OMFAQ was explicitly designed
    for purposes of clinical assessment,
    policy planning, and program evalu-
    ation.

2. The OMFAQ is a comprehensive measure,
    tapping five significant dimensions

TABLE 5.3

Comparison of Mean Ratings on Five Dimensions for Durham Community, Clinic, and Institutional Samples

Dimension	Community	Clinic	Institutional
Social Resources	2.24	3.26	4.20
Economic Resources	2.79	2.91	3.26
Mental Health	2.79	4.13	4.53
Physical Health	3.04	3.60	3.74
ADL	2.36	3.64	5.31

SOURCE: G.G. Fillenbaum, Valdiity and Reliability of the Multidimensional Functional Assessment Questionnaire. In Duke University Center for the Study of Aging and Human Development, Multidimensional Functional Assessment: The OARS Methodology, A Manual (second edition). Durham, NC: Duke University Center for the Study of Aging and Human Development, 1978, p. 29.

of functional status.

3. The OMFAQ has been demonstrated to
    be applicable to institutionalized
    older persons as well as community
    residents.

4. The reliability and validity of the
    OMFAQ have been demonstrated.

5. The combination of a comprehensive
    assessment of general functional
    status and a detailed description
    of service utilization provides a
    relatively unique opportunity for
    evaluating the effectiveness of
    service delivery.

In spite of these advantages, we encourage
deliberation among potential users of the OFMAQ.
The OMFAQ is neither easily administered nor
easily scored. The instrument is fairly long
and complex, requiring thoroughly trained interviewers and raters. To a large extent, the
reliability and validity of data based upon the
OMFAQ depend upon the skills of the interviewers
and raters. The OMFAQ is thus a highly attractive measure of general functional status, but
one which requires considerable commitment of
time and effort for optimal use.

Essential Reference

Duke University Center for the Study of Aging
    and Human Development. Multidimensional Func-
    tional Assessment: The OARS Methodology, A
    Manual, (second edition). Durham, North
    Carolina: Duke University Center for the
    Study of Aging and Human Development, 1978.

This manual is an' excellent reference for the OARS methodology, detailing such issues as the conceptualization and development of the OARS model; the reliability and validity of the instrument; guides to interviewing, data collection, and appropriate techniques of analysis; and presenting illustrations and applications of the OARS strategy.

STOCKTON GERIATRIC RATING SCALE

(Meer and Baker, 1966)

GERIATRIC RATING SCALE

(Plutchik et al., 1970)

Description of Instruments

Meer and Baker (1966) designed the Stockton
Geriatric Rating Scale (SGRS) to measure
"severity of impairment" among institutionalized
older persons. Impairment is measured in two
dimensions: physical disability and psychological facets of behavior. The SGRS consists of
33 items, which raters use to evaluate physical
and psychological impairment among institutionalized older persons. The authors indicate that
health care personnel (e.g., nurses, social
workers, attendants) are the most likely candi-
dates for raters; consequently the items have
been written to be easily understood and scored.
The SGRS is a behavioral rating scale--scores
are based solely upon the behavioral ratings of
observers, self-reports from subjects are not
solicited or recorded. Meer and Baker indicate
that the 33 items in the SGRS form four separate
impairment factors: Physical Disability, Apathy,
Communication Failure, and Socially Irritating
Behavior.
     Plutchik, Conte, Lieberman, Bakur, Grossman,
and Lehrman (1970) revised the SGRS to form a
28-item rating scale. Three items are identical
to those in the SGRS, 18 items tap the same concepts but have been reworded, and seven items

are new. Plutchik et al. call this instrument
the Geriatric Rating Scale (GRS).

We review both the SGRS and GRS.

Research Context and Use

   SGRS: Meer and Baker used three samples of
older patients in the development, refinement,
and validation of the SGRS. The first (1963
Sample) consisted of 692 male and female geriatric patients, age 65 and older. The second
sample (1965 Sample) included 489 male and female
geriatric patients, age 65 and older. Finally,
the New Admissions Sample consisted of 200 males
and females, age 65 and older, who were new
admissions to a geriatric ward. Individuals
with functional psychotic disorders as well as
with organic mental disease were represented in
each of the samples. The majority of work with
each sample was devoted to refining the SGRS and
to evaluating its reliability and validity. Meer
and Baker report normative data, including mean
scores on each item.

   Taylor and Bloom (1974) performed a cross-
validation study of the SGRS. Their sample consisted of 493 male and female geriatric patients,
all diagnosed as having organic brain disease,
and were significantly older (mean age=82.4 years)
than the patients in the Meer and Baker samples.
Taylor and Bloom do not report normative data.

   GRS: The GRS was developed and validated upon
a sample of 207 male and female geriatric patients
in a state hospital (Plutchik et al., 1970).
Total scores on the GRS represent degree of impairment, with higher scores representing greater

impairment. Plutchik et al. report the percent-
ile distribution of individual GRS scores in
their sample. The range of GRS scores was 0-51,
with a mean of 23.92 and a standard deviation of
10.20.

Smith, Bright, and McCluskey (1977) performed
a study to determine the factor structure of the
GRS. Their sample included 370 ambulatory male
and female patients in a psychiatric hospital.
The average age of the subjects was 74.26 years.
The three factors which emerged in factor analysis were: Withdrawal/Apathy, Antisocial Disruptive Behavior, and Deficits in Activities in
Daily Living. The sample mean for total scores
on the GRS was 20.84. Smith et al. also report
detailed normative data on the three factors.

Measurement Properties

Reliability. SGRS: For the four factor
scores and the total score, Meer and Baker report
internal consistency reliability estimates
ranging from .77 to .94. Examining inter-rater
reliability of the four factors and the total
scores, Meer and Baker report reliability estimates of .70 to .88, while Taylor and Bloom (1974)
report inter-rater reliability of .80 to .88.

GRS: For the total GRS score, Plutchik et al.
report inter-rater reliability of .87. Similarly,
Plutchik and Conte (1972) report inter-rater
reliability of .94.

For the three factors of the GRS, Smith et al.
report the following internal consistency reliability estimates: Withdrawal/ Apathy, .90; Antisocial Disruptive Behavior, .75; and Deficits in

Daily Living, .78.

Plutchik and Conte report a test-retest correlation of .65 on GRS total scores over a one-year interval. Similarly, Smith et al. report a test-retest correlation of .63 over a year for total scores and factor-specific test-retest correlations ranging from .32 to .65. Since significant change in functional status is likely during a year, these test-retest correlations appear appropriate.

In general, the results indicate that both the SGRS and the GRS exhibit adequate reliability.

Validity. SGRS: Taylor and Bloom (1974) report "significant" agreement between mean SGRS scores for given geriatric wards and supervisors' ratings of such wards (correlation unreported).

Meer and Baker (1966) present impressive evidence that the SGRS has predictive validity. Movement out of the hospital (discharge or visits) was significantly related to ratings on the SGRS, although Socially Irritating Behavior was less predictive than the other three factors.

GRS: Plutchik et al. (1970) report a correlation of .86 between psychiatric evaluation and individual GRS scores and a correlation of .95 between psychiatric evaluations and mean ward GRS scores.

Total GRS scores appear to significantly discriminate between geriatric and non-geriatric patients (Plutchik et al., 1970) and between organic and functional patients (Dastoor, Norton, Boillat, Minty, Papadopoulou, and Muller, 1975).

In addition, Plutchik and Conte (1972) provide some evidence that the GRS is a significant predictor of discharge for geriatric patients.

Sensitivity to Change. SGRS: Based upon Meer and Baker's (1966) study of SGRS factor scores before and after electro-shock therapy, the instrument appears sensitive to change and appropriate as a criterion variable in intervention studies.

GRS: The work of Plutchik and Conte (1972) provides limited evidence that the GRS also is sensitive to changes in physical and mental impairment.

Appropriateness for Older Samples. Both the SGRS and GRS appear appropriate for use with older persons, provided the observer-rater has been well trained. Plutchick et al.'s finding that the GRS discriminates between geriatric and non-geriatric patients suggests that the GRS may not be applicable to younger subjects.

Comments and Recommendations

Both the SGRS and the GRS appear to be effective measures of general impairment for use with samples of institutionalized older adults. The reliability and validity of both measures are well documented. In addition, the measures are potentially attractive criterion measures for use in intervention studies.

Several scoring methods have been used with both of these measures. In general, the use of separate factor scores appears preferable to the use of total scores. Meer and Baker indicate

that the factors may be correlated with and responsive to different variables. The use of
total scores thus could mask meaningful factor-
specific patterns.

We see no clear advantages which suggest use
of one scale rather than the other. The measures
are very similar and appear equally adequate.
The SGRS and GRS appear to be useful rating scales
for the functional assessment of geriatric
patients.

Essential References

Meer, B. and Baker, J.A. "The Stockton Geriatric
    Rating Scale." Journal of Gerontology, 1966,
    21, 392-403.

This article describes the development and
psychometric properties of the SGRS. In addition,
illustrations of the use of the SGRS in evaluating
intervention are presented.

Plutchik et al. "Reliability and Validity of a
    Scale for Assessing the Functioning of Geri-
    atric Patients." Journal of the American
    Geriatrics Society, 1970, 18, 491-500.

This reference describes the development and
psychometric properties of the GRS. Analyses to
determine the factor structure of the GRS are
described in:

Smith, J.M., Bright, B. and McCluskey, J.
    "Factor Analytic Composition of the Geriatric
    Rating Scale." Journal of Gerontology, 1977,
    32, 58-62.

TWENTY-TWO ITEM SCREEN SCALE

(Langner, 1962)

Description of Instrument

Mental illness is indexed by common types of psychiatric symptoms. Langner indicates that the screening scale provides a "rough indication of where people lie along a continuum of impairment of life functioning" (1962, p. 209). Although the issue of an appropriate cutting point has been debated heatedly, Langner clearly intended that the measure distinguish "sick" from "well."

The instrument consists of 22 items, describing common psychiatric symptoms. Response categories vary from question to question, but in general respondents agree or disagree that the symptoms are true of them. Most of the items in the Twenty-Two Item Screening Scale are taken from the Army Neuropsychiatric Screening Adjunct and the Minnesota Multiphasic Personality Inventory (MMPI).

Crandall and Dohrenwend (1967) suggest that four factors are included in the Twenty-Two Item Screening Scale: Psychological Symptoms, Psychophysiological Symptoms, Physiological Symptoms, and Ambiguous Symptoms. In his original article, Langner describes the items as tapping psychophysiological symptoms. In a recent article (Gersten, Langner, Eisenberg, and Orzek, 1974), Langner suggests that the scale may measure anxiety.

Research Context and Use

The Twenty-Two Item Screening Scale was developed in a large, social-epidemiological study of mental illness in Midtown Manhattan. The study was designed to ascertain the prevalence of mental illness and to determine the social correlates of psychological disorder. In addition to the use of self-report instruments, psychiatrists served as raters for the study. The Midtown Manhattan sample included 1,660 men and women, age 20-59. The mean score on the Twenty-Two Item Screening Scale was 2.83. Two books describe the study and research results in detail (Srole, Langner, Michael, Opler, and Rennie, 1962; Langner and Michael, 1963).

The Twenty-Two Item Screening Scale has been administered in numerous studies. Only major studies using the instrument are reported here.

In a validation study of the Twenty-Two Item Screening Scale, Manis, Brawer, Hunt, and Kercher (1963) administered the instrument to five samples: patients in receiving wards of a state mental hospital (mean=6.1), patients in the pre-discharge wards of a state mental hospital (mean=2.8), college students in a large, state university (mean=3.6), adult residents of a small rural community (mean 2.8), and adult residents of a large urban community (mean=3.2). More detailed normative data are presented in the Manis et al. (1963) article.

Crandall and Dohrenwend (1967) examined the factor structure of the Twenty-Two Item Screening Scale. They were particularly interested in the degree to which the instrument taps physical

rather than psychological illness and the implications of this for social class comparisons.
Their sample consisted of 1,710 men and women,
age 21 and over, from Washington Heights, New
York. The ethnic mix of the sample was purposely
diverse. Detailed normative data are presented
in their 1967 article.

Shader, Ebert, and Harmatz (1971) administered
the Twenty-Two Item Screening Scale to 241 persons
applying for out-patient psychiatric evaluation
at a mental health center. In this sample, the
mean number of symptoms reported was 8.3.

Meile (1972) administered the Twenty-Two Item
Screening Scale to 6,016 white men and women, age
20 and older, in three midwestern communities.
Detailed normative data for both total scores
and individual items are presented in his article.

Measurement Properties

Reliability. Very little evidence concerning
the reliability of the Twenty-Two Item Screening
Scale has been reported. Crandall and Dohrenwend
(1967) suggest that the instrument includes four
factors. Their evidence rests upon the judgments
of internists and psychiatrists, however, rather
than the results of factor analysis or other
statistical techniques.

Validity. There has been an impressive amount
of effort devoted to assessing the validity of
the Twenty-Two Item Screening Scale. The results,
however, are somewhat ambiguous.

Langner (1962) correlated scores on the Twenty-
Two Item Screening Scale with psychiatric ratings

of impairment for 1,660 individuals. The correlations ranged from .41 to .79. In a separate
substudy, Langner administered the instrument to
72 mentally healthy individuals and to 139 psychiatric patients. He reports that all 22 items
significantly discriminated between the two groups
at the .01 level. In a second, similar analysis,
the instrument was administered to 40 current
psychiatric outpatients (mean=4.78 symptoms),
182 former psychiatric patients (mean=4.20 symptoms), and 1,438 non-patients (mean=2.50 symptoms).
The means rank order as expected, with current
patients reporting the greatest number of
symptoms.

Manis et al. (1963) administered the Twenty-
Two Item Screening Scale to the five samples
described previously. The mean number of reported
symptoms for the groups rank order largely as
expected, the major anomaly being the low number
of symptoms reported by pre-discharge patients.
The authors report that the distributions of
scores for all the groups were widely dispersed,
however, blurring the results somewhat.

Manis et al. also correlated scores on the
Twenty-Two Item Screening Scale with the following variables in the two samples of psychiatric
patients described earlier: attendents' ratings,
participation in institutional activities, having
a grounds permit, number of previous admissions,
and length of hospitalization. All the correlations were significant and in the expected direction. In the sample of 1183 urban residents,
scores on the Twenty-Two Item Screening Scale
were correlated with scores on a "mental health
behavior scale," interviewers' ratings, and
reports of having ever received mental health

treatment. The correlations were significant: .65, .30, and .28 respectively.

Shader et al. (1971) report that the Twenty-Two Item Screening Scale is significantly related to several mental health measures: the Manifest Anxiety Scale (r=.77), the Cattell Anxiety Battery (4=.43), and a Neuroticism Scale (r=.72).

Dohrenwend and Crandall (1970) report mixed results in a known groups analysis. In their study, psychiatric outpatients, psychiatric in-patients, and non-patients were compared. Although non-patients had the lowest symptom scores, outpatients reported more symptoms than inpatients.

Muller (1971) reports that neurotics score higher than psychotic patients on the Twenty-Two Item Screening Scale.

Fink, Shapiro, Goldensohn, and Daily (1969) examined the referral process of patients pre-senting psychiatric disorder in general medical practice. Their results indicate that the higher the score on the Twenty-Two Item Screening Scale, the more likely the primary care physician was to refer the patient to a psychiatrist, rather than to treat the patient within the general medical care setting.

There is considerable evidence that the Twenty-Two Item Screening Scale is related to the exper-ience of life stress. Dohrenwend (1967) reports correlations between the scale and stressful life events ranging from .18 to .40, depending upon scoring method. Wildman and Johnson (1977) re-port a curvilinear relationship between screening scale scores and life events, with both an absence of events and numerous events related to higher symptom reports.

Sensitivity to Change. There is little empirical evidence concerning the measure's sensitivity to change.

Appropriateness for Older Samples. The sample upon which the Twenty-Two Item Screening Scale was developed excluded persons age 60 and older. Older respondents have been included in subsequent studies using the measure, although specific references to the instrument's applicablity to older subjects have not been reported. Given available evidence, the scale appears usable on older samples.

Comments and Recommendations

There are many unresolved issues concerning use of the Twenty-Two Item Screening Scale. Some of the most important issues are:

1. The appropriate cutting point for classifying respondents as "sick" or "well." Cutting points of four (Langner, 1962), seven (Meile, 1972), and ten (Manis et al., 1963), have been recommended previously.

2. Uncertainty as to whether the scale is intended to measure degree of mental disorder or the probability of suffering mental disorder.

3. Uncertainty as to what types of mental disorder are tapped by the instrument (i.e., is the measure

sensitive to both neuroticism and
psychosis).

4.   Uncertainty as to whether the scale
     is appropriate for use at the indi-
     vidual level or whether it is
     meaningful only for aggregate
     measurements.

Seiler (1973) has written a negative and fairly
persuasive case against the Twenty-Two Item
Screening Scale, referring specifically to the
above issues.

In all fairness to Langner, it should be noted
that he has urged caution in the use of the scale
and disclaimed its appropriateness for tapping
organic brain damage and mental retardation as
well as for classifying type of mental disorder.
More recently, he has suggested that the instrument may best be interpreted as a measure of
anxiety (Gersten, Langner, Eisenberg, Orzek,
1974).

In spite of all the negative features of the
scale, the evidence clearly indicates that the
instrument measures something related to mental
health. A clear distinction between "sick" and
"well" individuals is something that the scale
cannot provide. Nonetheless, used with appropriate caution, the instrument seems to warrant
further use and thoughtful attention. One of
the advantages of this measure is the vast amount
of validation effort that it has received. More
work is needed to determine its applicability
to older samples, however. Given that the measurement of mental illness by self-report instrument is a problematic endeavor, this instrument

appears to be one of the most attractive available.

Essential References

Langner, T.S.   A Twenty-Two Item Screening Score of Psychiatric Symptoms Indicating Impairment. Journal of Health and Human Behavior, 1962, 3, 269-277.

This reference describes the initial development of the instrument, its earliest applications, and efforts to establish its validity.

Manis, J.G., Brawer, M.J., Hunt, C.L., and Kercher, L.C.   Validating a Mental Health Scale. American Sociological Review, 1963, 28, 108-116.

This article describes a major study designed to validate the Twenty-Two Item Screening Scale and presents detailed normative data.

Seiler, L.H.   The Twenty-Two Item Scale Used in Field Studies of Mental Illness: A Question of Method, A Question of Substance, and A Question of Theory.   Journal of Health and Social Behavior, 1973, 14, 251-264.

This article provides a thoughtful, albeit critical, review of the measure, reviewing the results of numerous previous studies.

Chapter 6

SOCIOECONOMIC STATUS

CONCEPTUAL AND METHODOLOGICAL ISSUES

A good education, a respectable occupation, and a substantial income are all tangible symbols of success in our culture. In some sense, then, socioeconomic status (that is, possession of and access to these socially valued resources) must contribute to the quality of people's lives. As stated in a recent book on life quality, "there are many who would regard socioeconomic status and quality of life as almost stand-ins for each other" (Andrews and Withey, 1976, p. 294). Given only a statistical profile, few people would assess a person living in poverty with a low occupational status and little education as having a high quality of life. Similarly, people would probably express general agreement that a highly educated person of great wealth and in a prestigious occupation does have a high quality of life--on paper, at least.

Ultimately, however, "quality" remains a
highly subjective assessment. There are those
people who are "poor but happy" as well as those
for whom "money can't buy happiness." The relationship between possession of valued material
resources and subjective assessment of well-
being is far from perfect. Campbell, Converse,
and Rodgers (1976), for example, found a correlation of only .25 between income and satisfaction with financial situation. (p= .382)

Various social science theories propose the
contributions of socioeconomic status (SES) for
quality of life. The work of sociologists
studying inequality (or social stratification)
suggests that SES is important to quality of
life because it determines people's places in
the opportunity structure. SES not only defines
people's present positions but also has something to do with their "life chances" and those
of their children with regard to such valued
resources as power, friends, and prestige
(Miller, 1970). From a social psychological
standpoint, SES may be important to specific
aspects of psychological well-being (e.g., a
sense of security, accomplishment or self-
esteem) even if this is not clearly reflected
in measures of global life satisfaction (Kohn,
1969). From a public policy point of view, SES
also is related to the coping resources available
to individuals (U.S. Department of Health,
Education and Welfare, 1971).

Much empirical research has been conducted
to verify these notions and, by and large, these
studies confirm the central importance of SES
in many areas of American social life. Little
systematic attention, however, has been directed

to ascertaining the role which SES plays in the life of the older individual. While measures of SES are almost universally included as independent variables in gerontological studies, they frequently are regarded as peripheral to the research hypotheses or are examined outside of a theoretical context. Evidence of the low priority SES is given within gerontology can be found by comparing the haphazard measures of SES usually employed with some of the highly refined measures of life satisfaction. In that major changes in SES are likely to occur in late life, it seems appropriate to devote separate and special attention to issues of conceptualizing and measuring the SES of older individuals.

In this chapter, SES will be defined in terms of a standard sociological paradigm consisting of three components: occupation, education, and income. These components can be examined separately or as a combination of SES indicators. The quality of a person's life with regard to these dimensions can be determined both by the absolute quantity of these resources one possesses and by how one ranks on these dimensions relative to other people. Thus SES refers to both "state" and "status."

For the most part, the concepts and measures discussed in this chapter are those used in the study of the SES of the general population rather than for older people specifically. These concepts and measures are in wide use today and are becoming highly standardized across social surveys. In that there is no parallel standardized body of literature and research on the SES of the elderly, traditional concepts and measures provide the only solid starting

point for a discussion of SES in late life. As
will become apparent, many of these concepts and
measures require considerable modification for
use with older populations. Hopefully, this
analysis will stimulate thought which will lead
to development, refinement, and standardization
of concepts and measures better suited to the
elderly.

Occupation

As one central component of SES, occupation
plays an important role in orienting people's
attitudes and actions throughout life. To the
extent that it involves the continued practice
of a specific job or affiliation with a given
industry, occupation provides a source of personal identity and self-worth, an opportunity to
express skills, a structure for time, a circle
of associates and a regular income.

Occupation is also one source of social
standing. In major national studies, investigators have documented that (1) Americans per-
ceive some occupations to be of higher social
standing than others and (2) that people of dif-
fering social background generally concur as to
how various occupations rank with regard to
prestige (Reiss et. al., 1961; Hodge, Siegel and
Rossi, 1964). In many respects, then, occupation
conditions one's relative as well as absolute
well-being.

What significance does occupation have for
older people, a majority of whom are retired?
According to gerontological theory and research
on role loss in retirement, some occupational
benefits are lost after retirement (e.g. income

diminishes with the loss of earnings, contacts with work associates wane). But there is also evidence that retired people continue to identify themselves by their former occupation, for example, as a "retired schoolteacher" (Friedmann and Havighurst, 1954).

It is difficult to determine what significance occupation has for the social standing of older, retired people. Measures of occupational prestige are not designed to rank retired people. Use of these measures to assess the standing of a retired person requires the investigator to categorize a person by his former occupation. In order to modify current measures to deal with this issue, it will be necessary to determine whether people of all ages would rank a retired person by his former occupation, whether they would prefer to interpolate such categories as "retired physician" in current occupational prestige ratings or whether they would rank all retired people together. It would also be useful to discern whether retired persons continue to make status distinctions within their age group on the basis of occupation or whether they consider retirement a "leveler." Even if measures of occupational prestige are adjusted for these contingencies, further research should be conducted to determine the substantive significance that occupational prestige has for the broader life quality of older individuals including implications it has for social relationships.

Because a significant minority of older people remains in or rejoins the labor force, a thorough consideration of the impact of occupation on well-being in late life requires attention to "employment status" (i.e., employed versus unemployed versus retired). Through studies comparing the currently employed with unemployed and retired people of the same age, researchers could begin to isolate more of the effects of occupation on life experience.

Education

Although formal education is usually completed in one's early years, education is considered to be a determinant of life quality throughout life. Education leads to both tangible and intangible rewards: general knowledge and concepts with which to filter, organize and better understand events in the world around us, strategic learning and coping skills, technical skills which qualify a person for jobs and promotions, and prestige. Formal education is not the only way to attain these assets, however. Some colleges today recognize that life experiences can yield valuable knowledge and skills and therefore offer "college credit for things you learned in life."

What is the value of educational attainment in the life of an older person? The absolute value of early educational attainment may have diminished due to the obsolescence of knowledge and technical skills for today's world. Nevertheless, one's education may be a resource useful in old age for coping with life's contingencies. Level of education might determine the ease a person might have when faced with new situations which involve abstract reasoning or the mastery of new concepts (e.g., the writing of a will). On the other hand, a lifetime of experience might serve a person just as well. Education is

likely to play a minor role at best in contributing to the prestige of the older person, for
older people have relatively low levels of educational attainment compared to the population at
large. The National Opinion Research Center
(1976) reports the following mean educational
attainments of a large sample of Americans:

Age	Mean Educational Attainment
18-24	11.7 years
25-34	12.2
35-44	13.0
45-54	12.5
55-64	11.1
65-74	9.9
75-84	9.0
85+	8.4

Within the older population, however, differences
in education may be the source of status distinctions and have been shown to be a strong predictor of income-based status in late life
(Henretta and Campbell, 1976).

Educational attainment, defined as years
of formal education, is usally measured by a
single item such as "What is the highest grade
in school that you finished and got credit for?"
Although adequate for recording the formal educational attainments of older people, such traditional measures of education do not capture the
nuances of knowledge and skill gained through a
lifetime of experience. Although exceedingly
difficult to operationalize and measure, these
experience-based resources should not be overlooked when assessing the picture of the relative
quality of life of older individuals.

Income

Income, of course, is a significant indicator of life quality of people of all ages, for it can provide many of the comforts and protect against many of the discomforts life has to offer. Income has absolute value as a necessary sustaining element in self-maintenance and in raising a family. Income also offers relative rewards when others can ascertain a person's income from a display of "status symbols."

The financial picture of older individuals tends to look quite different from that of younger people. Whereas earnings contribute a significant and regularly replenishable portion of younger people's incomes, retirement drastically reduces the earnings of older people--on the average by about fifty percent (Streib, 1976). Age discrimination and debilitations of late life reduce the likelihood of reestablishing any significant earning potential.

With the loss of earnings, older people must look to new sources such as Social Security or private pension funds for income. For the most part, however, such income replacement plans do not fully compensate for the loss of earnings at retirement (Moon, 1977). Some forms of retirement income are regular and replenishable and tied into the cost of living to counteract the effects of inflation. Many pensions, however, are fixed and, with inflation, decline in purchasing value over time, creating a worsening situation for the older recipients in contrast to the rest of the population. For some older people, part of this income loss is offset by the transfer of in-kind income in the form of food stamps, Medicare and other social programs for the elderly as well as contributions from other family members.

Income is only one part of the individual's financial picture. Assets (e.g., owned homes, consumer durables, bank deposits, and stocks and bonds) and liabilities (e.g., loans) constitute another important part. The role assets play in determining the financial well-being of older people differs from that which they play in the lives of younger people. A person's net asset position or "net worth" (i.e., assets minus liabilities) tends to increase during years in the labor force so that people on the verge of retirement have greater valued assets than any other cohort in the population (Fisher, 1963). Older people are more likely to own mortgage-free homes and less likely to have significant liabilities than younger people (Lininger, 1963). Yet because of diminished income, older people are often forced to use liquid assets as income, thereby contracting their net asset position. One's financial picture can be greatly colored by the rate of this contraction, for in some cases, assets are insufficient to last one's lifetime. And there are, of course, many older people, especially among those with low incomes, who have few or no assets at all.

A well-rounded picture of the economic situation of the elderly individual requires consideration of both income and net worth. But in making the assumption that all assets could be converted into resources with equal value (the theory of potential income, Chen, 1966), we obtain a misleading estimate of the resources an individual has available for coping

with the cash-requiring contingencies of late
life. On the one hand, it may be desirable to
convert some assets, for in their present form
they may have lost their value to the owner.
Fisher (1963), for example, points out that older
people may wish to sell their homes purchased
much earlier in life because: "such homes no
longer suit the needs of many of their occupants.
The value of property investment will in some
instances be declining, while potential returns
from alternative investments are foregone"
(p. 112).

On the other hand, it may be impractical to
convert assets into disposable income. Many
assets maintain their greatest value to their
owner precisely in their material form. To a
certain extent, assets are pre-payments on the
expenses of late life (U.S. Department of Health,
Education and Welfare, 1971). For example, a
person whose home is paid off no longer has to
pay for shelter (beyond maintenance costs) and
a person who owns a washer and dryer does not
need to pay for laundry service. The cost of
replacing these commodities which are essential
to daily living is likely to be greater under
today's inflationary circumstances. These pre-
payments mean that current money resources are
not depleted on what would otherwise be unavoid-
able and perhaps sizeable expenses, but can
themselves hardly be considered sources of
disposable income.

Dollar value cannot capture the subjective
significance financial resources have for people,
sometimes of a magnitude that would preclude
converting assets into cash even to meet press-
ing needs. Although it is difficult to assess

the psychological value of owning one's home,
for example, or of having money in the bank,
both of these assets probably have special significance to older people. During a period of
life particularly fraught with losses and the
increased likelihood of dependency, a home and
a bank account can be equated with security,
independence from others, and freedom of choice--
cherished conditions which surely enrich the
quality of life.

This non-equivalence between money and the
personal value of what it buys highlights the
difficulties inherent in employing objective
indicators of the economic aspects of life
quality. In the quest for operational definitions of income adequacy, policy makers have
established some useful standards of comparisons
by which life quality can be gauged. The Federal
Poverty Index, for example, provides a sliding
scale of dollar amounts representing minimum
levels of living for individuals and for families
with different demographic characteristics.
Defined as an absolute and objective condition,
poverty theoretically can be alleviated by social
policies which transfer income to the needy until
incomes rise above poverty thresholds.

Some social scientists have proposed looking
at the adequacy of retirement income in relation
to a person's own pre-retirement income. This
pre- and post-retirement income differential is
operationally defined as the ratio of real income (i.e., income adjusted for inflation) for
the period under consideration to average real
income over the five years prior to retirement
(U.S. Department of Health, Education and Welfare, 1971). Presumably, such an indicator would

be sensitive to changes in life quality and standard of living. As Chen (1974) points out,

> since income inadequacy is a relative notion with social, psychological as well as economic dimensions, adequate retirement income might be expected to bear a 'reasonable relationship' to income before retirement in order to avoid feelings of 'relative deprivation.' (p. 135)

Policy makers have not yet agreed upon actual percentages which represent adequate earnings replacement levels for retired people or the appropriate level of social responsibility for providing partial replacement.

When gerontologists have turned to older people themselves for definitions of income adequacy, they have discovered wide variations in amounts specified, standards used to evaluate adequacy, and the degree to which inadequate income would cause dissatisfaction. Peterson (1969) cites some examples of different standards older people use to evaluate adequacy: comparison with retirees during the Depression, comparison with their own pre-retirement income, and adequacy to meet long-term future expenses.

Social Class

Social scientists have presented cogent arguments for considering income, occupation, and education jointly as well as separately. For one thing, their effects are highly interrelated. Theoretically, Andrews and Withey (1976) point out, for example, education

increases sensitivity and skills which give
entree to better jobs with higher incomes.   And
empirical research has reported strong correlations (Kohn, 1969; Andrews and Withey, 1976).
As used in contemporary American sociology, the
concept social class developed from the realiza-
tion that the three components hang together as
people cluster at different points in the social
structure.   So a social class is simply "an aggregate of individuals who occupy a broadly similar position in the scale of prestige" (Kohn,
1969, p. 10).   Most people are aware of the
existence of social classes and are able to
identify their place in a social class hierarchy.

Social class is an important variable in
determining people's attitudes and behaviors.
Its impact has been examined in sociological
studies of such diverse phenomena as fertility
patterns, political attitudes, religious behavior, values, and achievement motivation.   Social
class is thought to be highly contingent on occupation and education and, to a lesser degree,
income (Kohn, 1969).   The most widely used
measures reflect this weighting.

Conceptualized this way, however, social
class may not be highly useful for the study of
older people, for, as we have discussed, occupational prestige and formal educational attainment
tell us much less about older people than about
younger people.   Bloom (1972) proposes adding
income to measures of social class from which it
is excluded, for income, despite its limitations,
is still the most accurate single indicator of
well-being in relation to access to resources
for older people.

In that one's social class (traditionally conceived) tends to be determined in early adulthood and remain fairly stable over the life course, there is some uncertainty among investigators as to what effects should be expected to carry over into late life. One study (Bengtson, Cuellar, and Ragan 1977) discovered that social class is not a significant determinant of attitudes toward death. They cite age as "a leveler of prior social distinctions, as aging individuals of various walks of life deal with common biological imperatives of dying" (p. 87). Yet Henretta and Campbell (1976) report that midlife social class can be a predictor of late life net worth and that "over the lifetime of the individual, the effects of social class cumulate, since those of higher status, net of earnings differences, accumulate greater net worth" (p. 990). Further study is necessary to determine not only the extent to which blurring or accentuation of class distinctions is going on but also the domains of life in which each of these trends is occurring.

METHODOLOGICAL NOTE

There are some theoretically sound as well as practical reasons for collecting data in units other than the individual (cf. Moon, 1977; Morgan, 1965). For a number of economic variables (e.g., income, net worth), large scale social surveys do not ask individuals about their personal circumstances but rather ask about the couple, the family, or the household in that these form logical spending units. In addition, there are categories of people (e.g., wives who have no income of their own) whose personal income would provide misleading information about economic resources. On the other hand, reports of family or household income may obscure the poverty of an individual forced to live in that household for financial reasons. While ascertaining family or household income is the standard procedure for most purposes, for other purposes it might be useful to collect both family or household and individual incomes.

Similar issues come up in the measurement of occupational prestige and social class, both of which have been traditionally based on the attainments of the prototypical male head of household. Haug (1973) and Acker (1973) present convincing arguments for including data on the wife's attainment in order to make a more accurate assessment of the social standing of a family.

Thus, we should be sensitive to the unit of analysis incorporated in a given measure before interpreting research results and making cross-study comparisons.

COMMENTARY

It has become clear that many traditional concepts and measures of SES may be inappropriate for older people. Because we intuitively know that both economic and social positions remain important in late life, it is striking to note the extent to which the state of the art of SES conceptualization and measurement patently ignores the unique characteristics of older people.

Those people who have tackled these problems within gerontology have focused primarily
on improving income measures. Bloom (1972)
makes the argument that source of income makes
a better indicator of financial well-being than
any other proposed measure. Relatively easy to
ascertain, source of income yields information
beyond size of income, for it suggests something
about the stability of income over time and has
subjective ramifications.

What may be necessary, however, is a new
conceptualization of SES minimizing the contributions of education and occupation and substi-
tuting more relevant indicators of ability to
cope in late life. Certainly for policy-
planning or service-providing purposes, it becomes more important to develop measures which
examine the degree to which "absolute" basic
needs are taken care of rather than measures
which tap the more intangible gratifications of
"relative" social standing.

INSTRUMENTS TO BE REVIEWED

The instruments we review represent a broad
sampling from the wide range of SES measures currently in use. The North-Hatt Occupational
Prestige Ratings instrument (National Opinion
Research Center, 1947) is included because it is
a classic measure of occupational prestige, because it is simple to use, and because it was a
forerunner of the popular Duncan Socioeconomic
Index (1961a; 1961b), which also is reviewed.
Because income is a predominant indicator of
economic well-being in social research, a standard measure of income (U.S. Bureau of the Census,
1978) also is reviewed. As noted previously,

net worth is a theoretically significant aspect
of SES, frequently neglected when examining the
financial picture of elderly individuals.   Consequently, we included a discussion about the
measurement of net worth.   Poverty is a day-to-
day concern of many older persons as well as to
researchers and practitioners who work with the
elderly.   Consequently, we review the most common measure of poverty available--that used by
the federal government (U.S. Department of
Health, Education and Welfare, 1976).   And finally, the Hollingshead Two-Factor Index of Social Position (Hollingshead and Redlich, 1958)
is reviewed as an illustraiton of a social class
measure appropriate to and previously administered to older samples.

NORTH-HATT OCCUPATIONAL PRESTIGE RATINGS

(National Opinion Research Center, 1947)

Description of Instrument

The North-Hatt instrument lists 90 occupations and assigns them prestige scores based on popular perceptions of their general standing.

In using the instrument, the researcher need only inquire as to respondent's occupation and locate the occupational title on the ratings list to discern the prestige score.

Research Context and Use

In 1947, the National Opinion Research Center (NORC) undertook a study to determine how occupation contributes to social class distinctions. Principal investigators P. K. North and C. C. Hatt surveyed 2,920 Americans (in a quota sample from nine geographical regions, with three age groups: 14-20, 21-39 and 40 and over; and three socioeconomic groups) asking them to rate the standings of 90 occupations chosen from a wide range of white-collar and manual occupations.

Respondents were asked: "For each job mentioned, please pick out the statement that best gives your own personal opinion of the general standing that such a job has:

1.   Excellent standing

2.   Good standing

3.   Average standing

4.   Somewhat below average standing

5.   Poor standing   (Reiss et   al., 1961,
     p. 19)

A score of 100 was assigned to each excellent rating, 80 for good, 60 for average, 40 for somewhat below average, 20 for poor. A mean score was computed for each occupation from respondents' ratings. Average scores ranged from 33-96. The highest ranked occupation was Supreme Court Justice and the lowest shoe shiner. For a majority of occupations, respondents' social characteristics including age did not have a sizeable effect on rating   (Reiss et   al., 1961).

In 1956, A. Inkeles and P. H. Rossi utilized the North-Hatt format in a cross-cultural study of occupational prestige (Inkeles and Rossi, 1956). Comparing occupational prestige ratings in six industrial countries--the United States, Great Britain, Japan, New Zealand, Germany and the USSR--the researchers found very high correlations (often .9 or above) between the prestige scores of matched occupations for each pair of countries.

In 1963, NORC replicated the study with 651 respondents and discovered a correlation of .99 with the 1947 ratings (Hodge, Siegel and Rossi, 1964).

Some selected ratings for occupations in

1963 were as follows (Robinson, Athanasiou, and Head, 1969, pp. 360-361):

U.S. Supreme Court Justice	94
Physician	93
College professor	90
Banker	85
Minister	87
Dentist	89
Lawyer	88
Airline pilot	86
Public school teacher	81
Farm owner and operator	74
Electrician	76
Undertaker	74
Insurance agent	69
Policeman	72
Plumber	65
Barber	63
Restaurant cook	55
Filling station attendant	51
Bartender	48
Shoe shiner	34

There are no available data on the use of this instrument with older samples.

In recent years, the North-Hatt instrument largely has been replaced by the Duncan Socioeconomic Index (SEI) which evolved directly from the North-Hatt ratings. The Duncan SEI ranks hundreds of occupations and provides a regression equation by which additional occupations may be interpolated into the list, provided information on average education and income for that occupation is available.

Measurement Properties

Reliability. Reiss et al. (1961) report
that test-retest reliability is known to be
highest in the higher and lower extremes of the
prestige continuum and least reliable in the
mid-range. Reliability is lowered if a respondent is asked to rate unfamiliar occupations.

As noted above, NORC conducted a replication of their 1947 study and found a .99 correlation between scores from the two studies,
indicating a very high test-retest reliability
over a 25-year interval.

Validity. To our knowledge, the North-
Hatt ratings instrument has not been examined
for validity.

Sensitivity to Change. There is little
evidence of the instrument's sensitivity to
change since, to our knowledge, it has not been
longitudinally administered and analyzed. Theoretically, however, one's occupation, the item
by which one's prestige score is determined,
would be expected to be fairly stable for most
of the population.

Appropriateness for Older Samples. The
North-Hatt instrument can be applied to older
samples if the researcher collects data on major
lifetime occupations for retired people and is
willing to assume these titles are relevant for
the current social standing of respondents.

Comments and Recommendations

In that this instrument includes a limited

number of occupations, it may not be directly
applicable to many respondents. On the other
hand, its brevity and simplicity make for quick
reference.

Essential References

Reiss, A. J., Jr. et al., Occupations and Social
    Status. New York: The Free Press, 1961.

This volume details the development of the
North-Hatt instrument as well as the evolution
of the Duncan SEI from its origins in the North-
Hatt measure. This reference is recommended
instead of the original National Opinion Research Center article (1947) because it is more
widely available.

Robinson, J. P., Athanasiou, R., and Head, B.
    Measures of Occupational Attitudes and
    Occupational Characteristics. Ann Arbor,
    Michigan: Institute for Social Research,
    1969, pp. 360-361.

This reference is recommended for its clear
representation of the instrument in standard
form and its wide availability.

DUNCAN SOCIOECONOMIC INDEX

(Duncan, 1961)

Description of Instrument

The Duncan Socioeconomic Index (SEI) is designed to measure socioeconomic status as indicated by one's occupational rank. The index consists of an extensive list of occupations ranked according to the average number of years of education and average income characteristic of employees in those occupations.

To use the Duncan SEI, the researcher should acquire as much information about respondent's occupation as possible within the constraints of the study. Hauser and Featherman (1977) suggest asking the respondent what kind of work he does, what kind of business or industry he works in, whether he is self-employed or salaried, and whether he is employed in the public or private sector. With this information in hand, the researcher should attempt to assign the respondent a standard occupational title within a standard industry. Once the respondent's occupation has been categorized, the researcher can locate it on the Duncan SEI and look across to the corresponding score.

Research Context and Use

The Duncan SEI was an outgrowth of the North-Hatt Occupational Prestige Ratings. Duncan observed that the North-Hatt ratings included occupations which when taken together only

accounted for about half of the labor force.
Thus to achieve a picture of the broad American
occupational structure, Duncan developed a formula by which other occupations could be interpolated and ranked.

Duncan worked from 45 North-Hatt subjec-
tively-based occupational prestige scores and
1950 Census data to determine the weighted contributions income and education made to occupational prestige.   The regression equation is
(Duncan, 1961a, p. 124):

Prestige rating = .59 (education) +

.55 (income) - 6.0

Hauser and Featherman (1977) report that the
Duncan SEI was developed for all the occupations
in the U. S. Bureau of the Census publication,
Alphabetic Index of Occupations and Industries.

Henretta and Campbell (1976) employed the
Duncan as a measure of occupational attainment
in a study of the relationship between occupational and educational attainment in the pre-
retirement years and income after retirement.
The sample included 3,125 men aged 55-64 in 1962
and 209 men, aged 66-75, 66-76 and 68-77 in
1973, 1974 and 1975 respectively.   These groups
were drawn from probability samples of noninstitutionalized American males.   Occupational
category was obtained by asking retired respondents what type of work they "normally did."
The investigators found that occupational and
educational attainment were good predictors of
post-retirement income.   The authors concluded
that "the factors that determine income in

retirement are the same ones that determine income before retirement" (p. 990).

Bengtson, Cuellar and Ragan (1977) used the
Duncan SEI as a measure of social status in a
study of attitudes toward death among various
social groups. The sample included 1,269 individuals aged 45 and over from strata defined by
race, age, occupation, and sex. Socioeconomic
status, as measured by the SEI, was not a significant factor in predicting orientation to
retirement. Normative data are not available.

Measurement Properties

Reliability. Reliable use of the SEI requires that occupational titles be matched appropriately with the self-reports of respondents'
occupations. Ultimately, then, reliability depends upon the skill of the individual coding
the data. As Robinson et al. (1969) note,
this sort of occupational coding requires train-
ing and adequate cross-checking. McTavish (1964)
offers a variety of sound recommendations for
increasing the reliability of coding occupational
self-reports into SEI categories. For more recent and more detailed instructions on how to
categorize occupations reliably, see Hauser and
Featherman (1977, Chapter 2, pp. 51-80).

Validity. Duncan (1961b) found that the
correlation between the SEI and education is
.567 and the correlation between SEI and income
is .419, providing modest evidence of convergent
validity. Henretta and Campbell (1976) report
similar correlations on their sample of older
men: the correlation between SEI and education
was .54 and the correlation between SEI and

income was .38.   The SEI also exhibits convergent
validity with the Hollingshead Two-Factor Index
of Social Position: r = .89 (Kohn, 1969).

Sensitivity to Change.   There is little
evidence of the instrument's sensitivity to
change since, to our knowledge, it has not been
longitudinally administered and analyzed.   Theoretically, however, one's occupation, the item
by which one's SEI rating is determined, would
be expected to be fairly stable for most of the
population.

Appropriateness for Older Samples.   The
Duncan SEI can be applied to older samples if
the researcher collects data on major lifetime
occupations for retired people and is willing to
assume these titles are relevant for the current
social standing of respondents.

Comments and Recommendations

In that SEI score is derived directly from
occupation, data gathering should be more
straightforward than if serveral questions on
financial resources were also required to determine respondent's status.   Yet as Hauser and
Featherman (1977) point out, there are many
complexities in determining occupational categories.

Hauser and Featherman also report that using SEI scores for major occupational groups
yields a similar correlation to that obtained
by using detailed occupational scores.

Essential References

Duncan, O.D.   A Socioeconomic Index for All
     Occupations.   In A. J. Reiss, Jr. et al.,
     Occupations and Social Status.   New York:
     The Free Press, 1961a.

Duncan, O.D.   Properties and Characteristics
     of the Socioeconomic Index.   In A. J. Reiss,
     Jr. et al., Occupations and Social Status.
     New York: The Free Press, 1961b.

These references are recommended for their
straightforward presentations of the instrument
in standard form.   Research investigators who
already have coded occupations with the coding
scheme of the U.S. Bureau of the Census may prefer the Hauser and Featherman presentation of the
SEI which gives a score for each occupation in
the 1970 Census (1977, pp. 319-329).

MEASURE OF INCOME

(U.S. Bureau of the Census, 1978)

Description of Instrument

The U.S Bureau of the Census collects data
on income, defined as total family income from
all sources (before taxes), using a series of
questions about earnings, retirement benefits,
public assistance payments, income from assets,
cash contributions from relatives or friends,
and other income sources.   To determine total
income, the investigator must obtain dollar-
value responses to each question and sum them.
For some research purposes, however, source of
income is of concern.   In this situation, it
would be more useful to retain the individual
items as separate variables.

The facsimile questionnaire published in a
1978 Bureau of the Census report (U.S. Bureau of
Census, 1978, p. 226) indicates that total dollar amounts of money received in the last year
are obtained for the following sources:

--income from wages and salary
--income from nonfarm business, partnership,
  or professional practice
--income from an owned farm
--Social Security checks
--Railroad Retirement checks
--Supplemental Security Income checks from
  the federal, state, and/or local government
--public assistance or welfare by category

  (i.e., aid to families with dependent children)
  --interest on savings accounts, bonds, etc.
  --dividends
  --net rental income or royalties
  --estates or trusts
  --veteran's payments (excluding military retirement)
  --unemployment compensation
  --workmens compensation
  --private pensions and annuities
  --military retirement
  --other federal government employee pensions
  --state or local government employee pensions
  --alimony or child support
  --other regular contributions from persons not living in the household

The Census Bureau uses households, rather than the individual, as the unit of analysis. Consequently, the questions are asked of each household member and eventually summed not only across all sources, but also across all household members.

Research Context and Use

The U. S. Bureau of the Census periodically collects data on the income of the American population as part of their Current Population Survey of Households. The measure of household income has also been used in studies conducted by other branches of the federal government, including the Social Security Administration.

Recent data from the U.S. Bureau of the

Census (1978) reveal the relationship between age and income in the United States, as of 1976. Some of these data are presented in Table 6.1.

The Social Security Administration reports the distribution of income among the aged, shown in Table 6.2.

Table 6.2

Income Size: Percentage distribution of aged units 65 and older, by money income class, 1971

INCOME	All units
Number (in thousands)	15,637
Total percent	100
Less than $1,000	8
$1,000-$1,499	10
$1,500-$1,999	13
$2,000-$2,499	10
$2,500-$2,999	7
$3,000-$3,499	6
$3,500-$3,999	6
$4,000-$4,999	10
$5,000-$6,999	12
$7,000-$9,999	8
$10,000-$14,999	6
$15,000 and over	4
Median*	$3,071

*Median   is calculated from an income distribution with a finer breakdown.

ADAPTED FROM: S. Grad.   Income of the Population Aged 60 and Older, 1971. Wasington, D.C.:   Social Security Administration, Office of Research and Statistics.   HEW Publication No. (SSA) 77-11851. Staff Paper No. 26, 1977, p. 21.

Table 6.1

Percent Distribution of Families by Age of Householder
by Total Money Income in 1976

Age of Householder*	Number (thousands)	Percent Distribution				Median income (dollars)	Mean income (dollars)
		Total	Under $5,000	$5,000 to $19,999	$20,000 and over		
14 to 24 years	3,964	7.0	14.2	8.7	1.3	9,439	10,150
25 to 34 years	13,180	23.2	20.3	25.9	19.1	14,790	15,531
35 to 44 years	11,221	19.8	13.3	18.1	25.1	17,389	19,018
45 to 54 years	11,170	19.7	11.1	15.9	29.8	19,037	21,119
55 to 64 years	9,035	15.9	14.0	14.8	18.8	16,118	18,567
65 years and over	8,141	14.4	27.0	16.6	5.8	8,721	11,635

*The term "householder" will be replacing the terms "head of family" and "head of household" in the 1980 Census. The householder will be the first adult household member on the Census questionnaire.

ADAPTED FROM: U.S. Bureau of the Census. Table D: Percent Distribution of Families by Selected Characteristics, by Total Money Income in 1976. Money Income in 1976 of Families and Persons in the U.S., Current Population Reports. Consumer Income Series P-60 #114, Washington, D.C.: U.S. Department of Commerce, Government Printing Office, 1978, p. 6.

The Social Security Administration report also presents data on the income of the aged by source, as seen in Table 6.3.

Table 6.3

Income Sources: Percent of aged units 65 and older with money income from specified sources, 1971

Income source	All units
Number (in thousands)	15,637
Percent of units with -	
Earnings	31
Wage and salary	24
Self-employed	9
Retirement benefits	90
Social Security	87
Government employee pension	6
Private pension or annuity	17
Veteran's benefits	8
Unemployed insurance	1
Public assistance	10
Income from assets	49
Personal contributions	1

ADAPTED FROM: S. Grad. Income of the Population Aged 60 and Older, 1971. Washington, D.C.: Social Security Administration, Office of Research and Statistics. HEW Publication No. (SSA) 77-11851. Staff Paper No. 26, 1977, p. 25.

Measurement Properties

Reliability. There is a tendency for people to underestimate income from sources other than wages because they are more subject to faulty recall or to being overlooked entirely

(U.S. Department of Health, Education and Welfare, 1971).

Validity. No evidence of validity is presently available.

Sensitivity to Change. No evidence of sensitivity to change is presently available. It would be expected, however, that income reported in dollars would accurately reflect changes over time.

Appropriateness for Older Samples. This measure would be appropriate for all adults.

Comments and Recommendations

A question about income from sources other than earnings is certainly suitable for older people, for whom earnings constitute a small proportion of total income.

As noted in the text of this chapter, using the family as the unit of analysis can create special interpretive problems for researchers and respondents.

Essential References

U. S. Bureau of the Census. Money Income in 1976 of Families and Persons in the United States. Current Population Reports Consumer Income Series P-60 #114. Washington, D.C.: Government Printing Office, 1978.

This reference includes a facsimile of the March 1977 Current Population Survey questionnaire and reports detailed data for the U.S population in 1976.

MEASURE OF NET WORTH

(U.S. Department of Health, Education

and Welfare, 1971)

Description of Instrument

Net worth, defined as assets minus liabilities, is a dollar figure derived from respondents' estimations of liquid assets (those which
are readily convertible into cash, bank deposits,
stocks and bonds, loans to others, and the cash
value of life insurance policies), non-liquid
assets (not readily convertible into cash, including owned homes and other real estate as
well as owned businesses and the value of consumer durables and jewelry) minus liabilities
(debts).

To collect data on net worth, the researcher
should ask the respondent questions about home
equity (estimate of value of home minus present
value of mortgage), liquid savings (savings
account balance, estimate of stocks and bonds
value, and the value of savings bonds, other
bank deposits, or investments), business assets,
real estate, and debts (Henretta and Campbell,
1978). Optional items include equity in a pension plan or other forms of forced saving (e.g.,
life insurance).

Research Context and Use

Although a measure of net worth was included
in a national survey as far back as the 1963-64
Survey of Financial Characteristics of Consumers,

conducted by the Federal Reserve Board (reported in U.S. Department of Health, Education and Welfare, 1971), the inclusion of questions on assets and liabilities has not been widely adopted in social science research. Instead there has been a predominant reliance upon income as the sole indicator of economic well-being.

Table 6.4. presents the relationship between age and net worth, as reported in the 1963-64 Survey of Financial Characteristics of Consumers. The sample for this survey (n=2600) overrepresents high income families. Note that this skewness of the sample has a great effect on the net worth figures, such that the mean is consistently much higher than the median.

Table 6.4

Median Net Worth, Mean Net Worth, and Mean
Net Asset Position by Age of Family Head,
United States, 1962.

Age of Family Head	Median Net Worth	Mean Net Worth	Mean Net Asset Position*
Under 25	270	762	514
25-34	2,080	7,661	5,361
35-44	8,000	19,442	14,198
45-54	11,950	25,459	17,814
55-64	14,950	34,781	26,316
65 & Over	10,450	30,718	23,244

*Defined in this study as liquid assets minus liabilities.

SOURCE: U.S. Department of Health, Education and Welfare. Indicators of Status of the Elderly in the United States. Washington, D.C.: Government Printing Office, 1971, p. 51.

Table 6.5 presents data reported by the
Social Security Administration on the percentages
of older people who have specified types of
financial assets.

Table 6.5

Percent of Aged Units (age 65 and older)
with Specified Financial Assets, 1967

Type of Financial Asset	Percent
Any liquid assets	71
Money in banks	64
Money in credit unions	4
Money in savings and loan associations	22
Money in insurance policies	10
Other money assets	3
U.S. Savings Bonds	13
Stocks and corporate bonds	10
Loans or mortgages	4

ADAPTED FROM: L. E. Bixby et al. _Demo-
graphic and Economic Characteristics of the
Aged: 1968 Social Security Survey_. Washington, D.C.: Social Security Administration,
Office of Research and Statistics. HEW Publication No. (SSA) 75-11802, Research Report No.
45, 1974, p. 113.

More recently, Henretta and Campbell (1978)
determined respondents' net worth using data
collected in the National Longitudinal Survey
of Labor Force Participation. These investigators used the sample of older men, aged 50-64 in
1971. Their measure of net worth included both
liquid and non-liquid assets, but omitted equity
in pensions or other forms of forced savings.

The results indicated that age, family earnings,
occupational status, and marital status all are
significantly related to net worth. As would
be expected, persons who are middle-aged have
higher incomes and occupational status, and those
who are married have greater levels of net worth.

Measurement Properties

Reliability. Measurement of net worth is
reliable only to the extent that respondents
are able to accurately report asset and liability
figures. Thus, the measurement of net worth suffers from at least the same unreliability as
does the self-report of income--and perhaps more,
in that net worth is less likely to be discussed
in day-to-day conversations.

Validity. No data on the validity of net
worth measurement have been reported.

Sensitivity to Change. In theory, one's
net worth should increase over one's work life
and contract as assets are converted to disposable income during retirement.

Appropriateness for Older Samples. Net
worth is a highly appropriate measure of socioeconomic status for older people because it may
be a more accurate assessment of retired people's
financial situations than is income.

Comments and Recommendations

In that home equity constitutes the largest
non-liquid asset for most old people, some social
scientists suggest that a measure of liquid assets minus liabilities is a better indicator of

socioeconomic status, and certainly of resources available to meet the contingencies of late life. In some studies, this indicator is the referent for the term net asset position.

Henretta and Campbell (1978) empirically demonstrate that net worth is a preferable indicator of socioeconomic status than income/earnings and is more sensitive to variation in education and occupation.

If resources are available to collect data more complex than the usual estimates of income, ascertaining net worth is desirable.

Essential References

U.S. Department of Health, Education and Welfare. Indicators of Status of the Elderly in the United States. Washington, D.C.: Government Printing Office, 1971.

This reference provides a good overview of several indicators of financial well-being in late life, including net asset position or net worth. For a more detailed and insightful discussion of the use of net worth in the study of the life quality of older people, see:

Henretta, J. C. and Campbell, R. T. Net Worth as an Aspect of Status. American Journal of Sociology, 1978, 83, 1204-1223.

U.S. GOVERNMENT POVERTY MEASURE

(U.S. Department of Health, Education

and Welfare, 1976)

Description of Measure

Poverty can be defined as inadequacy with respect to a socially determined minimum standard of living. This index, which the federal government uses to measure poverty, is a listing of incomes which represent poverty thresholds for families adjusted for size, number of children, age and sex of household head, and farm versus non-farm residence. This index also is known as the Social Security Administration Poverty Index and the Orshansky Poverty Index.

The index consists of a series of cutoff points, which are poverty thresholds. The cutoff points in 1976 (the most recent year available) are presented in U.S. Bureau of the Census (1978).

Research Context and Use

Developed in 1965 by economist Mollie Orshansky, the index today is considered the standard federal poverty measure and is commonly used in the allocation of federal funds and in the determination of individual eligibility for social services.

The dollar amounts are updated annually in conjunction with changes in the Consumer Price

Index.   The dollar amounts are calculated by a
formula which assumes that food expenditures are
approximately one-third of one's budget.   The
numerical base, food expenditures, is estimated
as that minimum amount which would be necessary
to provide the individual with a nutritionally
sound diet.

People are defined as "poor" if income before taxes is below that noted as minimally
adequate for their circumstances.   Clark (1977)
reports that in 1974, 3.3 million individuals
age 65 and older--or 15.7% of the older popula-
tion--had incomes below the poverty level as
measured by this index.

The prospective user should note that the
poverty measure accomodates two units of analysis.   If the person lives alone, then the individual is the unit of analysis.   If the person
lives with others, the family living unit is the
unit of analysis. It also should be noted that the
definition of poverty varies according to the
age of the individual or household head.   Reflecting such items as increased medical costs,
the poverty level for persons age 65 and older
is somewhat lower than that for younger persons.

Measurement Properties

Reliability and Validity.   The reliability
and validity of the poverty index is contingent
upon the reliability and validity of the income
measure used.   In addition, since the Poverty
Index is recalculated yearly to adjust for
changes in the Consumer Price Index, it is important that the investigator utilize the current
cutoff points.   Since there is a significant lag

in publication of the poverty level thresholds, current standards must be requested directly from the U.S Bureau of the Census.

   Sensitivity to Change. In that poverty thresholds are posted as specific dollar amounts rather than ranges, the measure should be sensitive to changes over time in people's income. Furthermore, since the cutoffs are recalculated yearly, the Poverty Index also is sensitive to changes in the economic conditions of society which impact upon the economic well-being of individuals.

   Appropriateness for Older Samples. In that poverty thresholds have been adjusted along dimensions that have potential relevance for older individuals (size of household, age and sex of household head, etc.), this measure is appropriate for use with older samples.

Comments and Recommendations

   Use of the Poverty Index requires collection of data on income in sufficiently refined intervals to be useful for comparing against poverty thresholds in specific dollar amounts.

   As an indicator of the socioeconomic status of the elderly, the Poverty Index fails to take into account assets and in-kind income. A recent federal report (U.S. Department of HEW, 1976) reminds us: "It has been estimated that if food stamps were counted as income, the number of poor would decrease by 5 to 15% in 1974. Incorporating Medicare and Medicaid would also reduce the poverty count substantially if the definition of poverty remained unchanged.

Public housing, free school lunches, 'Meals on Wheels' for the aged, legal aid, neighborhood health centers and a long list of other in-kind social programs are other sources of resources for the poor." Thus, "this rise in in-kind benefits, many of them specifically aimed at reducing poverty, makes the current income measure used with the poverty line increasingly obsolete as a poverty performance measure, since it explicitly excludes the very programs instituted to reduce or alleviate poverty" (p. 32). It should be noted that the problem noted above is that the Poverty Index depends solely upon income, rather than the poverty thresholds per se.

The Poverty Index, as used with income as the sole determinant, thus has serious limitations as a measure of the total economic well-being of individuals. Because many government agencies and programs report their statistics using the Poverty Index, however, it may be of practical value.

Essential References

U.S. Department of Health, Education and Welfare. The Measure of Poverty. Washington, D.C.: Government Printing Office, 1976.

This volume details the history and current uses of the Poverty Index. It is an invaluable resource for anyone using the concept of poverty in research or planning.

HOLLINGSHEAD INDEX OF SOCIAL POSITION

(Hollingshead and Redlich, 1958)

Description of Instrument

The Hollingshead Index of Social Position
is designed to measure social class, conceptualized as a weighted combination of occupational
position and educational attainment. The index
ranks people along a five-point social class
scale, using self-report data on occupational
category and years of education. The investigator applies a prescribed formula to compute
weighted subscale scores and a resulting single
numerical value which represents social position.

To use the Hollingshead Index of Social
Position, the investigator must obtain respondents' occupations and years of education and
assign each respondent to one of seven occupational categories (scored 1-7, with 7 representing the least skilled) and one of seven educational categories (also scored 1-7, with seven
representing minimal educational attainment).
The occupational subscale score is multiplied
by seven, the education subscale score is multiplied by four, and the two products are summed
to obtain a single score which ranges from 11-17.
This single score then is used to classify the
respondent into one of five social class categories. The higher the single score, the higher
the social class (Bonjean et al., 1967).

Research Context and Use

In 1948, August B. Hollingshead and
Frederick C. Redlich developed a measure of
social class for a study of the relationship
between social class and mental illness (1958).
The measure of social class was developed and
standardized with extensive data from a cross-
sectional, random sample of 522 families in
New Haven, Connecticut.

As originally conceived, the Index of Social
Position represented a combination of three subscales, the occupational scale, the educational
scale, and the residential scale (rated on the
basis of address--the rationale being that where
one lives in the community tells something about
one's social position). Because of the difficulty in obtaining such residential ratings in
other communities, a two-factor version of the
index was developed and remains widely used
today as a measure of social class.

After developing the Index of Social Position, the investigators interviewed 3,559 residents of New Haven in a sample designed to be
representative of the American population as a
whole and determined that each social class exhibits distinct types and rates of mental
illness.

Lambing (1972) studied the relationship
between social class as measured by the two-
factor Index of Social Position and social
participation in a sample of 101 retired black
people in Gainesville, Florida. An availability
sample of retired professionals and retired
stable blue collar workers were added to a

representative sample taken from the Old Age
Assistance rolls of the Department of Public
Welfare consisting of people retired from service
occupations, domestic work and common labor.
Lambing found that there is a direct relationship
between social status and the number of leisure
time activities.

In a similar vein, Cutler (1973) used the
Index of Social Position to measure socioeconomic
status in a study of the relationship between
participation in voluntary associations and life
satisfaction in late life. The sample consisted
of 170 respondents 65 or older randomly selected
from the noninstitutionalized population of
Oberlin, Ohio. Cutler reports that the documented relationship between voluntary association participation and life satisfaction reflected the fact that people of higher socioeconomic status and in better health tend to
both participate in more activities and have
high life satisfaction. Bull and Aucoin (1975)
conducted a replication of Cutler's study using
a similar sample of 97 people in Kansas City,
reaching the same conclusion. Neither study
reports normative data with regard to social
class.

Measurement Properties

Reliability. Bonjean et al. (1967) report
that the Index of Social Position is reproducible
in the Guttman sense. That is, there is no over-
lap between education and occupation combinations.
Thus, if we know a person's single score, we
would be able to recover both the educational
level and occupational position.

Validity. Hollingshead and a second rater performed independent ratings of the social position of a subset of their sample (Hollingshead and Redlich, 1958). Ninety-six percent of the ratings were in agreement with the position assigned to the respondent on the basis of the Index of Social Position.

There also is evidence of convergent validity of the Index of Social Position. The multiple correlation of the index with education and occupation is .91 (Kohn, 1969). More important, Bonjean et al. (1967) report that the correlation between the Index of Social Position and the Duncan SEI is .89.

Sensitivity to Change. Thus far, the Index of Social Position has not been administered longitudinally; consequently, the measure's sensitivity to change cannot be assessed. Theoretically, however, since occupation and education tend to be established relatively early in life and remain stable, measures of social class are not expected to typically exhibit significant changes over time.

Appropriateness for Older Samples. The Index of Social Position can be applied to older samples if the investigator collects data on major lifetime occupation for retired people and is willing to assume that pre-retirement occupation is relevant for the current social standing of respondents.

Comments and Recommendations

The Index of Social Position is very easy to use in that it does not require data on income which is more difficult to obtain and less reliable. Bloom (1972), however, proposes revising the Index of Social Position to include a weighted component for income when using the measure on older samples.

In a critical review of the state of the art of social class measurement, Haug (1973) recommends the Hollingshead Index of Social Position because it provides a refined occupational breakdown in which "occupations are allocated to seven levels, ordered by the amounts of skill required and power possessed by job incumbents" (p. 88).

Essential References

Hollingshead, A. B. and Redlich, F. C. Social Class and Mental Illness. New York: John Wiley, 1958.

This reference details the development of the Index of Social Position and reports the findings of the classic study on the relationship between social class and mental illness.

Bonjean, C., Hill, R. and McLenore, S. Sociological Measurement. San Francisco: Chandler, 1967.

This reference presents the Index of Social Position in standard form in a concise, easy-to-understand manner.

Chapter 7

FINAL THOUGHTS AND FUTURE DIRECTIONS

Improving the quality of life may well become an explicit societal priority in years to come. Connoting idealistic sentiments, the phrase "quality of life" could become the basis of an alluring political bandwagon with wide public and scientific support. The very generality of the concept, however, makes it a problematic guide for effective policy planning. Policy makers must still determine what constitutes high life quality and whether a single definition can be broadly applicable in our diverse society. Once such definitional obstacles are overcome, funding priorities pose additional quandaries. Given the reality of scarce resources, advocates for such diverse programs as farm subsidies, higher education, and environmental protection—all of which might be viewed as contributing to quality of life—will undoubtedly find it necessary to compete for limited financial support.

As we have seen, social researchers also must confront the problem of pinning down the meaning (or meanings) of the concept quality of life in order to put hypotheses to scientific test. They must decide to what extent quality of life is to be viewed as an objective or a subjective phenomenon and isolate those aspects of social life for which discussion of quality (and change in quality) is theoretically meaningful. They then must come to terms with the paradoxical problems of developing quantifiable indicators of quality.

If quality of life is to be a useful organizing concept, it is in the mutual interest of policy makers and social researchers to establish a standardized body of working rules and tools for defining and measuring it. At the aggregate level, social indicators could be developed to assess both the conditions and the attitudes of the American public. At the individual level, such instruments could serve as tools for suggesting interventions suited to individual needs and evaluating the impact of such interventions.

The most useful indicators or measures are those for which conceptual referents have been precisely defined and psychometric properties have been well documented through application on large diverse samples in various research contexts. Unfortunately, many social science research instruments have not been subjected to the rigorous empirical evaluation and testing which permits recommending their use for policy and practice. Given our assessment of the state of the art of measuring life quality, today's policy maker would be advised to exercise caution in trying to draw definitive conclusions relevant

to policy decisions from social science research
employing many currently available instruments.

Yet the future of life quality measurement
holds much promise. Although there are gaps in
some substantive areas (e.g., measures of socioeconomic status of the elderly), there is a fer-
tile array of instruments being used in social
science research which need to be examined in
terms of our (or similar) criteria. If these
measures were used across studies with diverse
samples, normative data would be generated to
help the investigator interpret results. In developing adequate criterion measures for program
evaluation, strict attention should be given to
issues of sensitivity to change, validity, and
expecially in the present context, appropriateness
to older samples. Ideally, we look forward to
seeing catalogues of well-documented instruments
from which people can pick and choose those most
suitable for their specific purposes.

As refinement of measurement in this area pro-
ceeds, we anticipate that future research will
inform the definition and conceptualization as
well as the measurement, of life quality. The
four dimensions of life quality discussed in this
volume, for example, may be supplemented with
additional important dimensions. The relationships between and among dimensions of life quality
also could be profitably examined. For example,
is objective quality of life a prerequisite for
subjective assessment of life quality? Under
what conditions do people who rate low on life
quality as objectively measured, nonetheless
evaluate their subjective life quality in a positive manner? Finally, research which examines
the antecedents and consequences of life quality

will be an important area for future research.
If quality of life is to be an organizing rubric
for research, planning, and practice, the distribution, predictors, correlates, and implications of life quality will need to be carefully
delineated.

As we have consistently tried to show, the
concept of quality of life is ripe with possibilities for use in social research and practice.
We support and encourage efforts to assemble and
analyze promising instruments for the measurement
of life quality in the hope that they will promote the development of new and useful knowledge.

Bibliography

Acker, J. Women and Social Stratification: A Case of Intellectual Sexism. American Journal of Sociology, 1973, 78, 936-945.

Adams, D.L. Analysis of a Life Satisfaction Index. Journal of Gerontology, 1969, 24, 470-474.

Andrews, F.M. and Withey, S.B. Social Indicators of Well-Being. New York: Plenum Press, 1976.

Atchley, R.C. Respondents vs. Refusers in an Interview Study of Retired Women: An Analysis of Selected Characteristics. Journal of Gerontology, 1969, 24, 42-47.

Atchley, R.C. Selected Social and Psychological Differences Between Men and Women in Later Life. Journal of Gerontology, 1976, 31, 204-211.

Beiser, M. Components and Correlates of Mental Well-Being. Journal of Health and Social Behavior, 1974, 15, 320-327.

Bengtson, V.L., Cuellar, J.B., and Ragan, P.K. Stratum Contrasts and Similarities in Attitudes Toward Death. Journal of Gerontology, 1977, 32, 76-88.

203

Berger, E.   The Relations Between Expressed
    Acceptance of Self and Expressed Acceptance
    of Others.   Journal of Abnormal and Social
    Psychology, 1952, 47, 778-782.

Berger, E.   Relations Among Acceptance of Self,
    Acceptance of Others, and MMPI Scores.
    Journal of Consulting Psychology, 1955, 2,
    279-284.

Bigot, A.   The Relevance of American Life Satis-
    faction Indices for Research on British Sub-
    jects Before and After Retirement.   Age and
    Aging, 1974, 3, 113-121.

Bild, B.R. and Havighurst, R.J.   Life Satisfac-
    tion.   Gerontologist, 1976, 16, 70-75.

Binstock, R.H. and Shanas, E. (Eds.).   Handbook
    of Aging and the Social Sciences.   New York:
    Van Nostrand Reinhold Company, 1976.

Bixby, L.E.   et al.   Demographic and Economic
    Characteristics of the Aged: 1968 Social
    Security Survey.   Washington, D.C.:   Social
    Security Administration, 1974.

Bloom, M.   Measurement of the Socioeconomic
    Status of the Aged: New Thoughts on an old
    Subject.   Gerontologist, 1972, 12, 375-378.

Bloom, M.   The Paradox of Helping: Introduction
    to the Philosophy of Scientific Practice.
    New York: John Wiley, 1975.

Bohrnstedt, G.W.   A Quick Method for Determining
    the Reliability and Validity of Multiple -
    Item Scales. American Sociological Review,
    1969, 34, 542-548.

Bonjean, C., Hill, R., McLenore, S.   Sociological
    Measurement. San Francisco: Chandler, 1967.

Bortner, R.W. and Hultsch, F.   A Multivariate
    Analysis of Correlates of Satisfaction in
    Adulthood. Journal of Gerontology, 1970,
    25, 41-47.

Botwinick, J.   Cognitive Processes in Maturity
    and Old Age. New York: Springer, 1967.

Bradburn, N.M.   The Structure of Psychological
    Well-Being. Chicago: Aldine, 1969.

Bradburn, N.M. and Caplovitz, D.   Reports on
    Happiness: A Pilot Study of Behavior Related
    to Mental Health. Chicago: Aldine, 1965.

Bull, C.N. and Aucoin, J.B.   Voluntary Asso-
    ciation Participation and Life Satisfaction:
    A Replication Note. Journal of Gerontology,
    1975, 30, 73-76.

Bultena, G.   Life Continuity and Morale in Old
    Age. Gerontologist, 1969, 9, 251-253.

Busse, E.W. and Pfeiffer, E. (Eds.), Behavior
    and Adaptation in Late Life. Boston: Little,
    Brown, and Company, 1969.

Campbell, A., Converse, P.E., and Rodgers, W.L.
    The Quality of American Life. New York:
    Russell Sage Foundation, 1976.

Campbell, D.T., and Fiske, D.W.   Convergent and
    Discriminant Validation by the Multitrait-
    Multimethod Matrix.   Psychological Bulletin,
    1959, 56, 81-105.

Cantril, H.   The Pattern of Human Concerns.   New
    Brunswick, New Jersey: Rutgers University
    Press, 1965.

Carp, F.M.   Impact of Improved Housing on Morale
    and Life Satisfaction.   Gerontologist, 1975,
    15, 511-515.

Carp, F.M.   Morale: What Questions Are We Asking
    Of Whom?   In C.N. Nydegger (Ed.) Measuring
    Morale: A Guide to Effective Assessment.
    Washington, D.C.:   Gerontological Society,
    1977.

Chen, Y.   Economic Poverty: The Special Case
    of the Aged.   Gerontologist, 1966, 6, 39-45.

Chen, Y.   Retirement Income Adequacy.   In A.N.
    Schwartz and I. Mensh (Eds.), Professional
    Obligations and Approaches to the Aged.
    Springfield, Illinois: Charles C. Thomas,
    1974.

Clark, R.   Economics of Aging.   Tar Heel Econo-
    mist.   June. 1977.

Comptroller General of the United States.   The
    Well-Being of Older People in Cleveland, Ohio.
    Washington, D.C.:   General Accounting Office,
    1977.

Coopersmith, S.   The Antecedents of Self Esteem.
    San Francisco: W.H. Freeman, 1967.

Cottrell, W.F. and Atchley, R.C. Women in
    Retirement: A Preliminary Report. Oxford,
    Ohio: Scripps Foundation, 1969.

Crandall, R.C. The Measurement of Self-Esteem
    and Related Constructs. In J. Robinson and
    P. Shaver (Eds.), Measures of Social Psy-
    chological Attitudes (Revised Edition). Ann
    Arbor, Michigan: Institute for Social Re-
    search, 1973.

Crandall, R.C. An Exploratory Study of Self-
    Concept of Male Members of Selected Senior
    Centers in Southeastern Michigan. Disser-
    tation Abstracts, 1975, 28, 1824.

Crandall, D.L. and Dohrenwend, B.P. Some Re-
    lations among Psychiatric Symptoms, Organic
    Illness, and Social Class. American Journal
    of Psychiatry, 1967, 123, 1527-1537.

Cronbach, L.J. Coefficient Alpha and the Inter-
    nal Structure of Tests. Psychometrika,
    1951, 16, 297-334.

Cronbach, L.J. and Furby, L. Can We Measure
    Change--Or Should We? Psychological Bulletin,
    1970, 74, 68-80.

Cumming, E., Dean, R., and Newell, D.S. What is
    "Morale"? A Case History of Validity Problems.
    Human Organization, 1958, 17, 3-8.

Cumming, E. and Henry, W.E. Growing Old: The
    Process of Disengagement. New York: Basic
    Books, 1961.

Cutler, S.   Voluntary Association Participation
    and Life Satisfaction: A Cautionary Note.
    Journal of Gerontology, 1973, 28, 96-100.

Dastoor. D.P., Norton, S., Boillat, J., Minty, J.,
    Papadopoulou, F., and Muller, H.F.   A Psy-
    chogeriatric Assessment Program: Social
    Functioning and Ward Behavior.   Journal of
    the American Geriatric   Society, 1975, 23,
    465-469.

De Geyndt, W.   Five Approaches for Assessing
    Quality of Care.   Hospital Administration,
    1970, 15, 21-41.

Dohrenwend, B.P.   Social Status, Stress, and
    Psychological Symptoms.   American Journal of
    Public   Health, 1967, 57, 625-632.

Dohrenwend, B.P. and Crandall, D.L.   Psychiatric
    Symptoms in Community, Clinic, and Mental
    Hospital Groups.   American Journal of Psy-
    chiatry, 1970, 126, 1611-1621.

Dohrenwend, B.S.   Life Events as Stresses: A
    Methodological Inquiry.   Journal of Health
    and Social Behavior, 1973, 14, 167-175.

Dohrenwend, B.S. and Dohrenwend, B.P. (Eds.),
    Stressful Life Events: Their Nature and
    Effects.   New York: John Wiley, 1974.

Duke Center for the Study of Aging and Human
    Development.   Multidimensional Functional
    Assessment: The OARS Methodology (Second
    Edition).   Durham, North Carolina: Center
    for the Study of Aging and Human Development,
    1978.

Duncan, O.D.   A Socioeconomic Index for All
   Occupations.   In A.J. Reiss et al., Occu-
   pations and Social Status.   New York: The
   Free Press, 1961a.

Duncan, O.D.   Properties and Characteristics of
   the Socioeconomic Index.   In A.J. Reiss
   et   al., Occupations and Social Status.   New
   York: The Free Press, 1961b.

Edwards, N. and Klemmack, L.   Correlates of Life
   Satisfaction: A Re-examination.   Journal of
   Gerontology, 1973, 28, 497-502.

Epstein, S.   The Self-Concept Revisited: or a
   Theory of Theory.   American Psychologist,
   1973, 28, 404-416.

Ernst, M. and Kantor, R.   Cosmetics and the Institutionalized Woman.   Concern, 1976, April,
   19-22.

Fillenbaum, G.G.   Validity and Reliability of
   the Multidimensional Functional Assessment
   Questionnaire.   In Multidimenisional Func-
   tional Assessment: The OARS Methodology
   (Second Edition).   Durham, North Carolina:
   Center for the Study of Aging and Human.
   Development, 1978.

Fink, R., Shapiro, S., Goldensohn, S.S., and
   Daily, E.F.   The "Filter-Down" Process to
   Psychotherapy in a Group Practice Medical
   Care Program.   American Journal of Public
   Health, 1969, 59, 245-257.

Fisher, J.   Measuring the Adequacy of Retirement
    Incomes.   In H.L. Orbach and C. Tibbitts
    (Eds.), Aging and the Economy. Ann Arbor,
    Michigan: University of Michigan Press, 1963.

Fitts, W.   Tennessee Self-Concept Scale Manual.
    Nashville: Counselor Recordings and Tests,
    1965.

Fitts, W.   The Self-Concept and Psychopathology
    Nashville: Counselor Recordings and Tests,
    1972a.

Fitts, W.   The Self-Concept and Performance.
    Nashville: Counselor Recordings and Tests,
    1972b.

Fitts, W.   The Self-Concept and Behavior: Over-
    view and Supplement. Nashville: Counselor
    Recordings and Tests, 1972c.

Fitts, W. and Hammer, W.   The Self-Concept and
    Delinquency. Nashville: Counselor Recordings
    and Tests, 1969.

Friedmann, E.A. and Havighurst, R.J.   The Meaning
    of Work and Retirement. Chicago: University
    of Chicago Press, 1954.

Friedsam, H.J. and Martin, H.W.   A Comparison of
    Self and Physicians Health Ratings in an
    Older Population. Journal of Health and Human
    Behavior, 1963, 4, 179-183.

Gaitz, C.M. and Scott, J.   Age and the Measure-
    ment of Mental Health. Journal of Health and
    Social Behavior, 1972, 13, 55-67.

Gastil, R.   Social Indicators and Quality of
   Life.   Public Administration Review, 1970,
   30, 596-601.

George, L.K. and Maddox, G.L.   Subjective Adaptation to Loss of the Work Role: A Longitudinal Study.   Journal of Gerontology, 1977,
   32, 456-462.

Gersten, J.C., Langner, T.S., Eisenberg, J.G.,
   and Orzek, L.   Child Behavior and Life Events:
   Undesirable Change or Change Per Se?   In B.S.
   Dohrenwend and B.P. Dohrenwend (Eds.), Stress-
   ful Life Events: Their Nature and Effects.
   New York: John Wiley, 1974.

Gordon, C.   Self-Conceptions: Configuration of
   Content.   In C. Gordon and K. Gergen (Eds.),
   The Self in Social Interaction.   New York:
   John Wiley, 1968.

Gordon, C. and Gergen, K. (Eds.), The Self in
   Social Interaction.   New York: John Wiley,
   1968.

Gordon, G. and Morse, E.V.   Evaluation Research.
   In A. Inkeles (Ed.), Annual Review of Socio-
   logy, Volume I.   Palo Alto, California:
   Annual Review Inc., 1975.

Grad, S.   Income of the Population Aged 60 and
   Older, 1971.   Washington, D.C.:   Social
   Security Administration, 1977.

Graney, M.J.   Happiness and Social Participation
   in Aging.   Journal of Gerontology, 1975, 30
   701-706.

Grant, C.R.H. Age Differences in Self-Concept from Early Adulthood Through Old Age. Dissertation from University of Nebraska, 1966.

Gurin, G., Veroff, J., and Feld, S. Amercians View their Mental Health. New York: Basic Books, 1960.

Haug, M.R. Social Class Measurement and Women's Occupational Roles. Social Forces, 1973, 52, 86-98.

Hauser, R.M. and Featherman, D. The Process of Stratification: Trends and Analysis. New York: Academic Press, 1977.

Hausmann, R., Feldman, R.R. Hundert, J. and Davis, L. A Methodology for Evaluation of Quality of Life and Care in Long-Term Care Facilities. Chicago: St. Luke's Medical Center and Medicus Systems Corporation, 1974.

Havighurst, R.J. Successful Aging. In R.H. Williams, C. Tibbitts, and W. Donahue (Eds.), Processes of Aging. New York: Atherton Press, 1963.

Heise, D.R. Separating Reliability and Stability in Test-Retest Correlations. American Sociological Review, 1969, 34, 93-101.

Henretta, J.C. and Campbell, R.T.   Status At-
    tainment and Status Maintenance: A Study
    of Stratification in Old Age. American
    Sociological Review, 1976, 41, 981-992.

Henretta, J.C. and Campbell, R.T.   Net Worth
    as an Aspect of Status. American Journal of
    Sociology, 1978, 83, 1204-1223.

Heyman, D.K. and Jeffers, F.C.   Effect of Time
    Lapse on Consistency of Self-Health and Medi-
    cal Evaluation of Elderly Persons. Journal
    of Gerontology, 1963, 18, 160-164.

Hodge, R.W. Siegal, P.M. and Rossi, P.H.   Oc-
    cupational Prestige in the United States,
    1925-1963. American Journal of Sociology,
    1964, 73, 535-547.

Hoffman, A.M. (Ed.).   The Daily Needs and the
    Interests of Older People. Springfield,
    Illinois: Charles C. Thomas, 1970.

Hollingshead, A.B. and Redlich, F.C.   Social
    Class and Mental Illness. New York: John
    Wiley, 1958.

Hyman, H., Wright, C., and Hopkins, T.   Appli-
    cations of Methods of Evaluation. Berkeley,
    California: University of California Press,
    1962.

Inkeles, A. (Ed.), Annual Review of Sociology,
    Volume I. Palo Alto, California: Annual
    Review Inc., 1975.

Inkeles, A. and Rossi, P.H. National Comparisons
of Occupational Prestige. American Journal
of Sociology, 1956, 61, 329-339.

Jeffers, F.C. and Verwoerdt, A. How the Old
Face Death. In E.W. Busse and E. Pfeiffer
(Eds.), Behavior and Adaptation in Late Life.
Boston: Little, Brown, and Company, 1969.

Kalson, L. M*A*S*H*: A Program of Social Interaction Between Institutionalized Aged and
Adult Mentally Retarded Persons. Gerontologist, 1976, 16, 340-348.

Kaplan, H.B., and Pokorny, A.D. Self-Derogation
and Psychosocial Adjustment. Journal of
Nervous and Mental Disease, 1969, 149, 421-
434.

Kent, D., Kastenbaum, R., and Sherwood, S.(Eds.).
Research, Planning and Action for the Elderly.
New York: Behavioral Publications, 1972.

Kerckhoff, A.C. Family Patterns and Morale in
Retirement. In I.H. Simpson and J.C. McKinney
(Eds.), Social Aspects of Aging. Durham,
North Carolina: Duke University Press, 1966.

Kerlinger, F.N. Foundations of Behavioral Research. New York: Holt, Rinehart, and Winston, 1973.

Kerlinger, F.N. and Pedhazur, E,J. Multiple
Regression in Behavioral Research. New York:
Holt, Rinehart, and Winston, 1973.

Kilpatrick, F.P. and Cantril, H.   Self-Anchoring
    Scaling: A Measure of Individuals' Unique
    Reality Worlds. Journal of Individual Psy-
    chology, 1960, 16, 158-173.

Kish, L. Survey Sampling. New York: John Wiley,
    1965.

Knapp, M.R.J. Predicting the Dimensions of Life
    Satisfaction. Journal of Gerontology, 1976,
    31, 595-604.

Kohn, M.L. Class and Conformity. Homewood,
    Illinois: The Dorsey Press, 1969.

Kutner, B., Fanshel, D., Togo, A.M., and Langner,
    T.S. Five Hundred Over Sixty: A Community
    Survey on Aging. New York: Russell Sage
    Foundation, 1956.

Lambing, M.L.B. Leisure-Time Pursuit Among
    Retired Blacks by Social Status. Geronto-
    logist, 1972, 12, 363-367.

Langner, T.S. A Twenty-Two Item Screening Score
    of Psychiatric Symptoms Indicating Impairment.
    Journal of Health and Human Behavior, 1962,
    3, 269-277.

Langner, T.S. and Michael, S.T. Life Stress and
    Mental Health. New York: Free Press of
    Glencoe, 1963.

Lawton, M.P. The Dimensions of Morale. In D.
    Kent, R. Kastenbaum, and S. Sherwood (Eds.),
    Research, Planning and Action for the Elderly.
    New York: Behavioral Publications, 1972.

Lawton, M.P.   The Philadelphia Geriatric Center
   Morale Scale: A Revision.   Journal of Gerontology, 1975, 30, 85-89.

Lawton, M.P.   Morale: What are We Measuring?
   In C.N. Nydegger (Ed.), Measuring Morale:
   A Guide to Effective Assessment.   Washington,
   D.C.:   Gerontological Society, 1977.

Lawton, M.P., Ward, M., and Yaffe, S.   Indices
   of Health in an Aging Population.   Journal
   of Gerontology, 1967, 22, 334-342.

Lemon, B.W., Bengtson, V.L., and Peterson, J.A.
   An Exploration of the Activity Theory of Aging:
   Activity Types and Life Satisfaction Among
   In-Movers to a Retirement Community.   Journal
   of Gerontology, 1972, 27, 511-523.

Lininger, C.A.   Some Aspects of the Economic
   Situation of the Aged: Recent Survey Findings.
   In H.L. Orbach and C. Tibbitts (Eds.), Aging
   and the Economy.   Ann Arbor, Michigan: University of Michigan Press, 1963.

Lohmann, N.   Correlations of Life Satisfaction,
   Morale, and Adjustment Measures.   Journal of
   Gerontology, 1977, 32, 73-75.

Louis Harris and Associates.   The Myth and Reality of Aging in America.   Washington, D.C.:
   National Council on Aging, 1975.

Lowenthal, M.F., Thurnher, M., and Chiriboga, D.
   Four Stages of Life.   San Francisco: Jossey-
   Bass, 1975.

Lyons, M. Cognition and Affect in Social Psychology: The Case of Self-Esteem. Presented at Annual Meeting of Southern Sociological Society, 1977.

Maddox, G.L. Some Correlates of Differences in Self-Assessment of Health Status Among the Elderly. Journal of Gerontology, 1962, 17, 180-185.

Maddox, G.L. Activity and Morale: A Longitudinal Study of Selected Elderly Subjects. Social Forces, 1963, 42, 195-204.

Maddox, G.L. Persistence of Life Style among the Elderly: A Longitudinal Study of Patterns of Social Activity in Relation to Life Satisfaction. In B.L. Neugarten (Ed.), Middle Age and Aging. Chicago: University of Chicago Press, 1968.

Maddox, G.L. and Douglass, E.B. Self-Assessment of Health: A Longitudinal Study of Elderly Subjects. Journal of Health and Social Behavior, 1973, 14, 87-93.

Maddox, G.L. and Wiley, J. Scope, Concepts, and Methods in the Study of Aging. In R.H. Binstock and E. Shanas (Eds.) Handbook of Aging and the Social Sciences. New York: Van Nostrand Reinhold Co., 1976.

Manis, J.G., Brawer, M.J., Hunt, C.L., and Kercher, L.C. Validating a Mental Health Scale. American Sociological Review, 1963, 28, 108-116.

Mason, K.O., Mason, W.M., Winsborough, H.H., and
    Poole, W.K.   Some Methodological Issues in
    Cohort Analysis of Archival Data.   American
    Sociological Review, 1973, 38, 242-258.

McTavish, D.G.   A Method for More Reliably Coding
    Detailed Occupations into Duncan's Socio-
    economic Categories.   American Sociological
    Review, 1964, 29, 402-406.

Mechanic, D.   Medical Sociology: A Selective
    View.   New York: The Free Prees, 1968.

Meer, B. and Baker, J.A.   The Stockton Geriatric
    Rating Scale.   Journal of Gerontology, 1966,
    21, 392-403.

Meile, R.L.   The Twenty-Two Item Index of Psy-
    chophysiological Disorder: Psychological or
    Organic Symptoms.   Social Science and Medicine,
    1972, 6, 125-135.

Miller, D.C.   Handbook of Research Design and
    Social Measurement.   New York: David McKay
    Company, Inc., 1970.

Monge, R.H.   Developmental Trends in Factors
    of Adolescent Self-Concept.   Developmental
    Psychology, 1973, 8, 382-393.

Monge, R.H.   Structure of the Self-Concept from
    Adolescence Through Old Age.   Experimental
    Aging Research, 1975, 1, 281-291.

Moon, M.   The Measurement of Economic Welfare:
    Its Application to the Aged Poor.   New York:
    Academic Press, 1977.

Morgan, J.N. Measuring the Economic Status of the Aged. International Economic Review, 1965, 6, 1-17.

Morgan, J.N. and Smith, J.D. Measures of Economic Well-Offness and Their Correlates. American Economic Review, 1969, 59, 912-926.

Moriwaki, S.Y. The Affect Balance Scale: A Validity Study with Aged Samples. Journal of Gerontology, 1974, 29, 73-78.

Morris, J.N. Changes in Morale Experienced by Elderly Institutional Applicants Along the Institutional Path. Gerontologist, 1975, 15, 345-349.

Morris, J.N. and Sherwood, S. A Retesting and Modification of the Philadelphia Geriatric Cneter Morale Scale. Journal of Gerontology, 1975, 30, 77-84.

Muller, D.J. Discussion of "Langner's Psychiatric Impairment Scale: A Short Screening Device". American Journal of Psychiatry, 1971, 128, 601.

Murray, J.M. (Ed.). Journal of Katherine Mansfield. London: Constable and Company, 1927.

National Center for Health Statistics. Health in the Later Years of Life. Washington, D.C.: Government Printing Office, 1971.

National Opinion Research Center. Jobs and Occupations: A Popular Evaluation. Opinion News, 1947, 9, 3-13.

National Opinion Research Center. National Data Program for the Social Sciences: Codebook for the Spring 1976 General Social Survey. Chicago: University of Chicago, 1976.

Nehrke, M.F., Actual and Perceived Attitudes Toward Death and Self-Concept in Three-Generational Families. Paper presented at 27th Annual Meeting of the Gerontological Society, 1974.

Nehrke, M.F., Hulicka, I.M., and Morganti, J.B. The Relationships of Age to Life Satisfaction, Locus of Control, and Self-Concept in Elderly Domiciliary Residents. Paper presented at 28th Annual Meeting of the Gerontological Society, 1975.

Neugarten, B.L. (Ed.), Middle Age and Aging. Chicago: University of Chicago Press, 1968.

Neugarten, B.L. Successful Aging in 1970 and 1990. In E. Pfeiffer (Ed.), Successful Aging: A Conference Report. Durham, North Carolina: Center for the Study of Aging and Human Development, 1974.

Neugarten, B.L., Havighurst, R.J., and Tobin, S.S. Measurement of Life Satisfaction. Journal of Gerontology, 1961, 16, 134-143.

Nunnally, J.C. Psychometric Theory. New York: McGraw Hill, 1967.

Nydegger, C.N. (Ed.). Measuring Morale: A Guide to Effective Assessment. Washington, D.C.: Gerontological Society, 1977.

Omwake, K.   The Relation Between Acceptance of
    Self and Acceptance of Others as Shown by
    Three Personality Inventories.   Journal of
    Consulting Psychology, 1954, 18, 443-446.

Orbach, H.L. and Tibbits, C. (Eds.), Aging and
    the Economy.   Ann Arbor, Michigan: Univer-
    sity of Michigan Press, 1963.

Osgood, C.E. and Suci, G.J.   Factor Analysis of
    Meaning.   Journal of Experimental Psychology,
    1955, 50, 325-328.

Osgood, C.E., Suci, G.J., and Tannenbaum, P.
    The Measurement of Meaning.   Urbana, Illinois:
    University of Illinois Press, 1957.

Palmore, E. and Kivett, V.   Change in Life Satis-
    faction: A Longitudinal Study of Persons Aged
    46-70.   Journal of Gerontology, 1977, 32, 311-
    316.

Palmore, E. and Luikart, C.   Health and Social Fac-
    tors Related to Life Satisfaction.   Journal
    of Health and Social Behavior, 1972, 13, 68-
    80.

Patrick, D.L., Bush, J.W., and Chen, M.M.   To-
    ward an Operational Definition of Health.
    Journal of Health and Social Behavior, 1973,
    14, 6-23.

Peterson, D.A.   Retirees' Views on Income Ade-
    quacy.   In The Aging Consumer.   Ann Arbor,
    Michigan: The University of Michigan-Wayne
    State University Institute on Gerontology,
    1969.

Pfeiffer, E. (Ed.), Successful Aging: A Con-
    ference Report. Durham, North Carolina:
    Center for the Study of Aging and Human
    Development, 1974.

Pfeiffer, E. (Ed.), Multidimensional Functional
    Assessment: The OARS Methodology, A Manual
    (First Edition). Durham, North Carolina:
    Center for the Study of Aging and Human
    Development, 1975.

Plutchik, R. and Conte, H. Change in Social and
    Physical Functioning of Geriatric Patients
    over a One-Year Period. Gerontologist, 1972,
    12, 181-184.

Plutchik, R., Conte, H., Lieberman, M., Bakur,
    M., Grossman, J., and Lehrman, N. Reliability
    and Validity of a Scale for Assessing the
    Functioning of Geriatric Patients. Journal
    of the American Geriatric Society, 1970, 18,
    491-500.

Postema, L.J. Reminiscing, Time Orientation and
    Self Concept in Aged Men. Dissertation,
    Michigan State University, 1970.

Reiss, A.J. et al. Occupation and Social Status.
    New York: The Free Press, 1961.

Reynolds, W.J., Rushing, W.A. and Miles, P.L.
    The Validation of a Function Status Index.
    Journal of Health and Social Behavior, 1974,
    15, 271-288.

Rice, D.P., Anderson, A., and Cooper, B.S.
Personal Health Care Expenditures of the
Aged and Nonaged, Fiscal Years 1966 and 1967.
Washington, D.C.: Government Printing Office,
1968.

Riley, M.W. Aging and Cohort Succession: In-
terpretations and Misinterpretations. Public
Opinion Quarterly, 1973, 37, 35-49.

Riley, M.W. and Foner, A. Aging and Society,
Volume One: An Inventory of Research Findings.
New York: Russell Sage Foundation, 1968.

Robinson, J.P., Athanasiou, R., and Head, B.
Measures of Occupational Attitudes and Occu-
pational Characteristics. Ann Arbor, Michigan:
Institute of Social Research, 1969.

Robinson, J. and Shaver, P. (Eds.). Measures
of Social Psychological Attitudes. Ann Arbor,
Michigan: Institute for Social Research,
1969.

Robinson, J. and Shaver, P. (Eds.). Measures
of Social Psychological Attitudes. (Revised
Edition). Ann Arbor, Michigan: Institute
for Social Research, 1973.

Rosenberg, M. Society and the Adolescent Self-
Image. Princeton, New Jersey: Princeton
University Press, 1965.

Rosencranz, H.A. and Pihlblad, C.T. Measuring
the Health of the Elderly. Journal of Gerontology, 1970, 25, 129-133.

Rosow, I. Socialization to Old Age. Berkeley, California: University of California Press, 1974.

Rosow, I. Morale: Concept and Measurement. In C. Nydegger (Ed.), Morale: A Guide to Effective Assessment. Washington, D.C.: Gerontological Society, 1977.

Schaie, K.W. A General Model for the Study of Developmental Problems. Psychological Bulletin, 1965, 64, 92-107.

Schwartz, A.N. An Observation on Self-Esteem as the Linchpin of Quality of Life for the Aged: An Essay. Gerontologist 1975, 15, 470-472.

Schwartz, A.N. and Mensh, I. (Eds.). Professional Obligations and Approaches to the Aged. Springfield, Illinois: Charles C. Thomas, 1974.

Scitovsky, T. The Joyless Economy. New York: Oxford University Press, 1976.

Seiler, L.H. The Twenty-Two Item Scale Used in Field Studies of Mental Illness: A Question of Method, A Question of Substance, and a Question of Theory. Journal of Health and Social Behavior, 1973, 14, 251-264.

Selltiz, C., Wrightsman, L.W., and Cook, S.W. Research Methods in Social Relations (Third Edition). New York: Holt, Rinehart, and Winston, 1976.

Shader, R.I., Ebert, M.H., and Harmatz, J.S.
  Langner's Psychiatric Impairment Scale: A
  Short Screening Device. American Journal of
  Psychiatry, 1971, 128, 88-93.

Shanas, E. The Health of Older People. Cambridge, Massachusetts: Harvard University
  Press, 1962.

Shaver, P. Measurement of Self-Esteem and Related Constructs. In J. Robinson and P.
  Shaver (Eds.). Measures of Social Psychological Attitudes. Ann Arbor, Michigan:
  Institute for Social Research, 1969.

Sheldon, E.B. and Moore, W.E. (Eds.), Indicators
  of Social Change: Concepts and Measurement.
  New York: Russell Sage Foundation, 1968.

Silber, E. and Tippett, J. Self-Esteem: Clinical Assessment and Measurement Validation.
  Psychological Reports, 1965, 16, 1017-1071.

Simpson, I.H., Back, K.W., and McKinney, J.C.
  Attributes of Work, Involvement in Society,
  and Self-Evaluation in Retirement. In I.H.
  Simpson and J.C. McKinney (Eds.). Social
  Aspects of Aging. Durham, North Carolina:
  Duke University Press, 1966.

Simpson, I.H. and McKinney, J.C. (Eds.). Social
  Aspects of Aging. Durham, North Carolina:
  Duke University Press, 1966.

Smith, J.M., Bright, B., and McCluskey, J. Factor Analytic Composition of the Geriatric
  Rating Scale. Journal of Gerontology, 1977,
  32, 58-62.

Srole, L.   Measurement and Classification in
   Socio - Psychiatric Epidemiology: Midtown
   Manhattan Study (1954) and Midtown Manhattan
   Restudy (1974).   Journal of Health and Social
   Behavior, 1975, 16, 347-364.

Srole, L., Langner, T.S., Michael, S.T., Opler,
   M.K., and Rennie, T.A.C.   Mental Health in the
   Metropolis: The Midtown Manhattan Study.
   New York: McGraw Hill, 1962.

Streib, G.   Morale of the Retired.   Social Problems, 1956, 3, 270-276.

Streib, G.F.   Social Stratification and Aging.
   In R.H. Binstock and E. Shanas (Eds.).   Hand-
   book of Aging and the Social Sciences. New
   York: Van Nostrand Reinhold Company, 1976.

Suchman, E.A., Phillips, B.S., and Streib, G.F.
   An Analysis of the Validity of Health
   Questionnaire.   Social Forces, 1958, 36, 223-
   252.

Sullivan, D.F.   Conceptual Problems in Developing
   an Index of Health.   Health and Vital Statistics, Series 2, No. 17.   National Center for
   Health Statistics. Washington, D.C.: U.S.
   Government Printing Office, 1966.

Sze, W.C. and Hopps, J.G. (Eds.).   Evaluation
   and Accountability in Human Service Programs.
   Cambridge, Massachusetts: Schenkman, 1974.

Taylor H.G. and Bloom, L.M.   Cross-Validation
   and Methodological Extension of the Stockton
   Geriatric Rating Scale.   Journal of Gerontology, 1974, 29, 190-193.

Thompson, W., Correlates of the Self Concept.
Nashville, Tennessee: Counselor Recordings
and Tests, 1972.

Tippett, J. and Silber, E.   Self-Image Stability:
The Problem of Validation. Psychological
Reports, 1965, 17, 323-329.

Tissue, T.   Another Look at Self-Rated Health
Among the Elderly. Journal of Gerontology,
1972, 27, 91-94.

Trimakas, K., and Nicolay, R.C.   Self-Concept
and Altruism in Old Age. Journal of Gerontology, 1974, 29, 434-439.

U.S. Bureau of the Census. Money Income in 1976
of Families and Persons in the United States.
Washington, D.C.: Government Printing Office,
1978.

U.S. Department of Health, Education, and Welfare.
Indicators of Status of the Elderly in the
United States. Washington, D.C.: Government
Printing Office, 1971.

U.S. Department of Health, Education, and Welfare.
Strategy for Research for Long-Term Care of
the Elderly. Washington, D.C.: Government
Printing Office, 1972.

U.S. Department of Health, Education, and Welfare.
The Measure of Poverty. Washington, D.C.:
Government Printing Office, 1976.

U.S. Public Health Service. Limitation of
Activity Due to Chronic Conditions. Washington, D.C.: Government Printing Office, 1972.

Ward, R.A. The Impact of Subjective Age and
    Stigma on Older Persons. Journal of Geron-
    tology, 1977, 32, 227-232.

Webster's New World Dictionary of the American
    Language (College Edition) New York: The
    World Publishing Company, 1968.

Wells, L.E. and Marwell, G. Self-Esteem.
    Beverly Hills, California: Sage Publications,
    1976.

Wildman, R.C. and Johnson, D.R. Life Change and
    Langner's Twenty-Two Item Mental Health Index:
    A Study and Partial Replication. Journal of
    Health and Social Behavior, 1977, 18, 179-188.

Williams, R.H., Tibbits, C.,and Donahue, W. (Eds.).
    Processes of Aging. New York: Atherton Press,
    1963.

Wolk, S. Situational Constraint as a Moderator
    of the Locus of Control-Adjustment Relation-
    ship. Journal of Consulting and Clinical
    Psychology, 1976, 44, 420-427.

Wolk, S. and Telleen, S. Psychological and
    Social Correlates of Life Satisfaction as a
    Function of Residental Constraint. Journal
    of Gerontology, 1976, 31, 89-98.

Wood, V., Wylie, M.L., and Sheafer, B. An
    Analysis of a Short Self-Report Measure of
    Life Satisfaction: Correlation with Rater
    Judgment. Journal of Gerontology, 1969, 24,
    24, 465-469.

World Health Organization. World Health Organi-
    zation Charter. Geneva: World Health Organi-
    zation, 1946.

Wylie, M.L. Life Satisfaction as a Program
    Impact Criterion. Journal of Gerontology,
    1970, 25, 36-40.

Wylie, R. The Self-Concept. Lincoln, Nebraska:
    University of Nebraska Press, 1974.

Ziller, R., Hagey, J., Smith, M.D., and Long, B.
    Self-Esteem: A Social Construct. Journal of
    Consulting and Clinical Psychology, 1969, 33,
    84-95.

INDEX